Funky stitches

Funky
Stitches

–Anita Plant–

- Fun ideas for embroidery projects -

Dedicated to André, Emma and David.

AUTHOR'S ACKNOWLEDGEMENTS

First of all I would like to say a big thank you to all the staff at Metz Press for believing in my idea and running with it! To Wilsia and Ilse for always being there at the end of a telephone and to Lindie for her great book design. I would also like to thank David for his unwavering camera shots and for keeping a cool head during the photo shoots.

Thanks also to Janice at DMC for supplying lists of stockists and yarn for photographs.

Thank you to my friend Richard and his staff at ACG for supplying me with bedlinen and muslin curtains often at short notice and allowing me to rummage amongst their offcuts. To Bronwyn for her feedback on the various designs and for giving me lots of gingham! I would also like to thank Natalie for telling me to "go for it" when I first bounced the idea off her and for her constructive comments, even if she thinks my tea-cosy looks like Napoleon's hat! To my dear friend Jane for all her enthusiasm on my behalf and to Sue for her long-distance encouragement. Thanks also to Catherine for the loan of her lap-top. To my parents-in-law, Rex and Hulda for all their love and support.

I really cannot find enough words to thank my parents, without whom this book would have been way past its deadline. Thank you Mum and Dad for endless fetching and carrying of children, for the loan of the sewing machine and for being great parents and grandparents. To my children, Emma and David, for being an endless source of love, joy and inspiration.

Last, but by no means least, to my husband, André, who had to endure my (occasional) theatrical artistic outbursts (which generally had something to do with the sewing machine). Thanks for your artist's eye and constructive criticism, for your wonderful stitch illustrations, and for your enthusiasm, support and encouragement from start to finish of this book. And thanks for stepping in to take over the domestic duties and for being a great husband and father. I love you.

Published by Metz Press
Unit 106, Hoheizen Park 1, Hoheizen Crescent,
Hoheizen 7530 South Africa
First edition 2002
Copyright © Metz Press 2002
Text copyright © Anita Plant
Photographs & illustrations © Metz Press

Publisher & editor	Wilsia Metz
Sub-editor	Kobie Ferreira
Design & lay-out	Lindie Metz, jack
Photography	David Pickett, Alchemy Foto Imaging
Illustrator	André Plant
Production	Ilse Volschenk & Andrew de Kock
Reproduction	Cape Imaging Bureau, Cape Town
Printing and binding	Tien Wah Press, Singapore
ISBN	1-875001-71-9

Contents

Introduction

Embroidery has been used for many centuries to enhance ordinary household items, from tea cloths to bed linen. Sadly, in the rush of modern-day life where everything is mass-produced, embroidery has become something of a lost art, but it's certainly making a come-back.

My own interest began in earnest after the birth of my first child, Emma, six years ago. While breast-feeding and simultaneously flicking through a magazine I came across a simple embroidery project for a sheet or a blanket. I decided to try it and was amazed by several things: how therapeutic I found the simple act of stitching to be, how easy it was, and how beautiful the finished product was.

I was hooked. The possibilities of embroidery became endless, and I began to work out my own fun and funky designs, drawing inspiration from urban graffiti to nature. As my daughter became older and more artistic her drawings have been a constant source of ideas. Friends received embroidered presents and before long I was commissioned to embroider for other people. This led me to start a small embroidery business, dealing mainly in bed linen, and soft furnishings. I produced a sample book containing swatches of designs and used this to market myself through retail outlets and craft markets. Before I knew it I was making money out of my hobby!

Over the years many people have asked me about the designs and how to reproduce them for themselves. Many don't believe me when I tell them how simple it really is. This has led me to write *Funky stitches*.

The aim of this book is to show how simple, yet effective, embroidery can be. I have included some of my most popular designs in a series of room-by-room projects. There is also a section with some useful ideas for gifts. Most of the designs are very versatile and can be used on a variety of different articles. The designs are both contemporary and fun and the stitches are simple and clearly illustrated.

Most of all I hope that this book will act as inspiration for you to create your own designs. Have fun!

Materials and equipment

One of the things I like about embroidery is how little equipment you actually need. I also find that it's a very portable craft and I have often taken my embroidery along on long car journeys, to my daughter's swimming and ballet lessons, or wherever I know I will be waiting and have time to spare.

BASIC EQUIPMENT

Embroidery hoop

This consists of two wooden or plastic hoops that fit one inside the other. Lay the fabric to be embroidered over the smaller hoop and place the larger hoop over the top. Pull the fabric taut and even and tighten the screw on the larger hoop. This ensures that the fabric is kept stretched.

There are many different sizes available, so choose one that is comfortable for your hand-size. Some stitches, particularly those worked along a border, can be worked without a hoop.

Needles

The most commonly used needle for embroidery is a crewel needle. These needles are available in a range of sizes from 1 to 10 — the higher the number, the smaller the needle. I generally use a size 5 or 6. Check that the eye of the needle is large enough for the embroidery cotton to pass through without splitting, but not so thick that it leaves a hole in the fabric when it's passed through.

Scissors

You will need a pair of small, sharp and pointed embroidery scissors for cutting thread. Also useful is a larger pair for cutting fabric, and zig-zag scissors or pinking shears. I use these as a shortcut when sewing seams together, as they prevent the edges from fraying. You can also use them when cutting out shapes for appliqué to prevent fraying.

Embroidery thread

You can use almost any thread for embroidery, from silk to wool, depending on the effect you wish to create. For a delicate effect, such as the antennae of a butterfly, I use ordinary sewing cotton; for a thicker more textured appearance, as on the woolly sheep, I use wool or all six strands of a twisted thread. Stranded cottons are most commonly used for embroidery. They come in a wide range of colours, which is updated each year. Coton Perlé is not a stranded thread, so it cannot be split, but it gives a thicker, satin-like appearance, and is available in different thicknesses.

For the projects in this book I used the DMC range of cottons. In each project three strands of thread are used, unless specified otherwise. When you buy the cotton you will see that it is made up of six strands. This is generally too thick, so I usually cut the length I require and then split it in half as I need it.

Water-soluble marker pen

Such a pen is essential for tracing or drawing the design onto the material.

Tape-measure and set square

These are essential for placing designs accurately.

Thimble

This is a matter of preference. A thimble can save your fingertips if you are doing a lot of embroidery, but I have never got used to using one.

MATERIAL

Basically, anything can be embroidered onto, apart from a very loosely woven material. It all depends on what the finished item is going to be used for, and how often it will be washed. It also depends on the type of design you are embroidering. For example, if you are using thicker threads you can use a textured fabric, but for fine lines and details a smoother fabric would be better.

My own preference is to use 100% cotton or linen, especially for bed-linen. The ACG suppliers listed on page 96 will make up items to your specifications. They also supply duvet-covers and pillowcases, as well as bed-linen in plain white cotton and coloured polyester-cotton. I use a lot of white as I find the designs show up beautifully.

You don't necessarily need to buy new linen, especially if you are not sure how it will look. So scour second-hand, antique and junk shops for good, used linen. I find the quality of old sheets wonderful, as they are generally made with a tighter weave, which makes them ideal for embroidery. With a good hot wash they look as good as new. You can sew them together to make up duvet covers, or use them for table-cloths, curtains, cushions, throws and so on. If you are feeling adventurous, dye them to match existing colour schemes. You can also use polyester-cotton, which is cheaper and available in a wide range of colours.

Mattress ticking is great to use and is very versatile.

For cushions, I use a lot of calico and linen, or cotton and linen blends, but anything is possible really. It is also a good idea to pre-wash this type of fabric so that any shrinkage that occurs will occur before you begin embroidering.

Voile is a lovely fabric for embroidery. Transferring the design can be a bit tricky as voile has a tendency to move, but if you have another person to help it is fine. It is well worth a try, as the finished effect of embroidery on this sheer fabric is stunning.

You can also embroider on waffle cotton, towelling and T-shirt material. I often embroider my own designs onto plain T-shirts. This really gives a unique garment that you know nobody else will be wearing.

Gingham is fun to use. You can embroider onto white and then appliqué the patches onto gingham, or appliqué gingham onto white and combine this with embroidery. I have used these combinations in projects in this book. So keep favourite scraps of fabric, however small, as you never know when an idea will present itself.

TRANSFERRING THE DESIGN

Most of the designs in this book are simple enough to be drawn freehand onto the fabric with a water-soluble pen. But if you don't feel confident enough to do this, use dressmaker's carbon paper. First photocopy the template, enlarging or reducing as you wish, then:

- Iron the fabric smooth and place it right side up on a flat hard surface.
- Put dressmakers carbon paper face down on the fabric where you want the design to go and secure it with masking tape. Place the design over the paper and tape it in position.
- Use a fine ballpoint pen to trace over the design, pressing hard. Once you have drawn over the design, remove the papers.

If the fabric is sheer enough you can place it over the template and trace the design directly onto it with a water-soluble pen. Alternately, use a window as a light source. First trace the design onto a piece of paper and stick it onto a window. Tape your fabric in position over the drawing and trace. Once you have finished embroidering, wash the fabric to remove any residue of carbon or water-soluble pen.

GOOD LIGHTING

I am often asked if my eyes don't get tired. It is with this in mind that I always sew in good lighting. I use a tall angle-poise lamp when sewing in the evenings or when it's overcast. The flexible arm allows me to angle the light onto the work. Do not be tempted to sew in sunlight as the UV light will damage your eyes.

If my eyes do get tired, I use this simple yoga exercise to refresh them. Rub your hands together to generate some heat and then cup them over each eye, blocking out any light. Stare into the darkness for a minute or two. You'll be amazed at how refreshing this is.

Use this also after driving for long periods, or working at a computer.

STARTING AND FINISHING OFF

Traditionally the only knots used in embroidery are French ones. So, when starting and finishing off a piece of work the loose cottons are *sewn in*. This is important when the back is likely to be on show, as is the case with serviettes. Here's how I do it.

When *starting*, bring the thread out at the front of the work, leaving a length of about 2,5 cm (1 inch) at the back of the fabric. As you begin making your stitches, catch this loose end down with your first few stitches.

When *finishing off*, the end of the thread is passed through the back of the last few stitches on the wrong side of the work. This ensures the last stitches are secure and look neat. Now cut off any excess cotton.

When starting a new design I often first do it on a scrap piece of fabric to make sure I'm happy with the colours and stitches to avoid having to unpick. But if the unthinkable happens and you do have to unpick, carefully snip each wrong stitch with your embroidery scissors and pull out the cut ends with tweezers.

When starting a new skein of thread, cut off a small length and tie it through the band with the colour's number on it. Keep it safe as a record for future reference, (or in my case, for when I have run out of thread and my husband has to collect it for me!). It also enables you to phone your local stockist first to check if they have that particular colour in stock.

I specified thread colours for all the projects in the book. But the DMC range is vast, and you should change the colours for specific items to suit your décor and taste. The swatches on the right are of the colours used for projects featured and give you an idea of what is available.

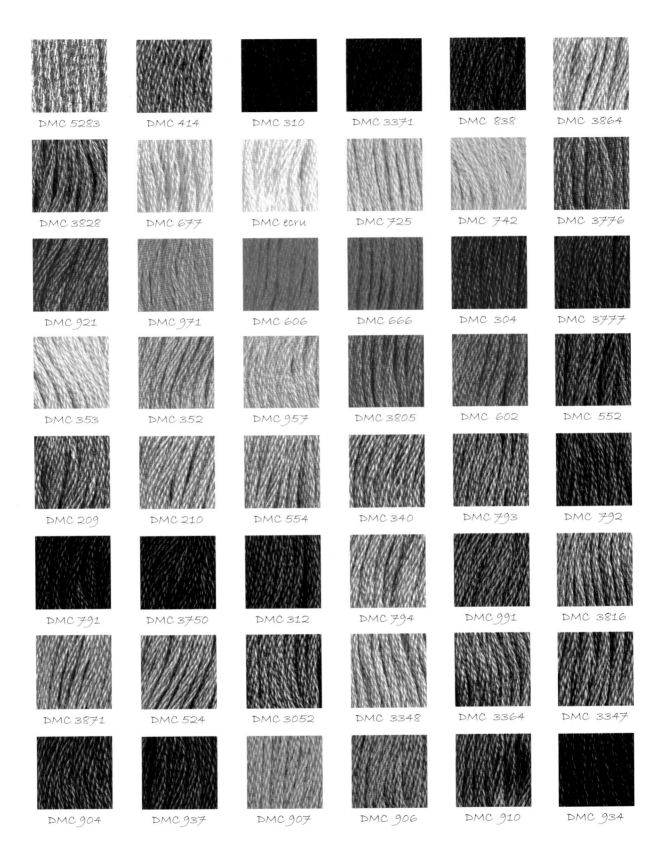

DMC 5283   DMC 414   DMC 310   DMC 3371   DMC 838   DMC 3864

DMC 3828   DMC 677   DMC ecru   DMC 725   DMC 742   DMC 3776

DMC 921   DMC 971   DMC 606   DMC 666   DMC 304   DMC 3777

DMC 353   DMC 352   DMC 957   DMC 3805   DMC 602   DMC 552

DMC 209   DMC 210   DMC 554   DMC 340   DMC 793   DMC 792

DMC 791   DMC 3750   DMC 312   DMC 794   DMC 991   DMC 3816

DMC 3871   DMC 524   DMC 3052   DMC 3348   DMC 3364   DMC 3347

DMC 904   DMC 937   DMC 907   DMC 906   DMC 910   DMC 934

Lavender & dragonfly duvet-cover

Lavender is one of my favourite herbs to embroider. It is quick and easy and I love the colour combination of the soft purple-blue flower heads and cool grey-green stems.

This ready-made plain duvet-cover in white cotton has been embroidered with a mixture of lavender and dragonflies. The dragonflies scattered among the lavender are fun and pretty and the delicate lacy effect on the wings is deceptively easy to reproduce. The theme can be carried over onto pillowcases, continental pillowcases, laundry-bags, curtains, towels, and anything else you can think of.

YOU WILL NEED

I plain white duvet cover
Templates of lavender and dragonfly
Water-soluble pen
Tape-measure
Crewel needle size 6
Embroidery hoop
Small, sharp scissors

DMC embroidery thread for lavender

3 skeins 793 cornflower blue
2 skeins 524 light fern green

DMC embroidery thread for dragonfly

1 skein 793 cornflower blue
1 skein 3817 light celadon green
1 skein 414 steel grey
Black sewing cotton

The number of skeins needed depends on how many motifs you embroider. I hate running out of thread in the middle of a project, so I have been generous with the skein allowances.

Lay out your duvet cover on a flat surface and use a water-soluble pen to mark where you want the embroideries to go.

For a project this size it is useful to make several photocopies of the designs, cut them out and play around with the positioning. I generally use 17-20 motifs on a queen-size duvet.

Use a tape-measure to ensure that the spacing between motifs is equal. Take care over the layout, as positioning mistakes are easy to change at this stage by using a clean damp sponge to erase the pen marks.

Once you are happy with the placement, transfer the design either by tracing it through the cover, drawing it on freehand, or using carbon-paper (see page 10).

For the lavender, using 3 strands of DMC 524, embroider the stem in stem stitch. The stems on this design are intertwined on top of each other, so it helps to do one stem at a time. When you get to a leaf position, divert and embroider the leaf, using fishbone stitch.

Change to 3 strands of DMC 793 and embroider the petals, using lazy daisy stitch.

For the dragonfly, using 3 strands of blue, embroider the head and abdomen in raised satin stitch. Keep the stitches small and even. Make the head slightly wider than the body. Take ordinary black sewing cotton and sew the 2 leg-sections in straight stitch. Sew each eye as a French knot. Secure the thread by sewing it into the stitches of the dragonfly's head.

Taking 3 strands of DMC 3817, sew the top wing, using couched satin stitch. Once you have gone around the outline of the wing, use the same colour and number of threads to embroider the lacy inset in straight stitches. Secure the thread by sewing it into the abdomen.

Change to DMC 414 and repeat the process for each bottom wing.

Once completed, wash and iron.

I have found that the easiest way to iron a duvet cover is on the bed itself. But protect the mattress underneath with another sheet, preferably one that needs ironing too!

Lavender sprigs on Oxford pillowcase

I embroidered small pretty sprigs of lavender around the border of a ready-made Oxford pillowcase (a pillowcase with an extra border around the outside) to go with the duvet cover. They will look equally effective scattered over the centre of a pillowcase or cushion.

You will need

1 ready-made Oxford pillowcase (look for one with a nice wide border for ease of working)
Template of lavender sprigs
Water-soluble dressmaker's pen
Tape-measure
Crewel needle size 6
Embroidery hoop
Small sharp embroidery scissors

DMC embroidery thread in the following colours

1 skein 793 cornflower blue
1 skein 524 light fern green

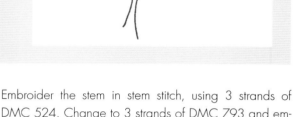

Use a water-soluble pen to mark the position of the lavender sprigs, measuring carefully with a tape-measure to ensure that they are equally spaced. Transfer the design as explained on page 10.

Embroider the stem in stem stitch, using 3 strands of DMC 524. Change to 3 strands of DMC 793 and embroider each lavender head using lazy daisy stitch.

Repeat for the rest of the sprigs.

Ladybird & leaf on pillowcases

To add variety to the main bedroom linen I embroidered a leaf design on a blue pillowcase, using a combination of stem and chain stitch. The ladybird adds humour to this contemporary design. Don't be put off by the number of different stitches used, as this is really a very easy design.

You will need

- 1 pair of pillowcases
- Template of leaf and ladybird
- Water-soluble pen
- Crewel needle size 6
- Embroidery hoop
- Sharp scissors

DMC embroidery thread

- 1 skein ecru
- 1 skein 209 dark lavender

Transfer the design by tracing it through the pillowcase, drawing it on freehand, or using carbon-paper (see page 10). If you are embroidering a pair of pillowcases for a double bed, make sure the design is on the left of one and the right of the other so that when the pillows are placed on the bed, the design lies on the outer edge (this may sound obvious, but I have made this mistake before!).

For the leaf, place the pillowcase in your hoop and use 3 strands of DMC ecru to embroider the stem, following the curve of the line in stem stitch and moving your hoop along as you go. Try to keep the stitches small and even. Once completed, use the same colour to embroider each leaf outline in chain stitch. Start and finish at the bottom of the leaf. Using the same thread, embroider the veins of the leaf in fern stitch, finishing off at the top of the leaf. Continue to do each leaf in the same way. When embroidering anything that has a rounded shape that needs to be filled in, I generally run a small line of stitches around the outline as a guide.

To embroider the ladybird, start with 3 strands of DMC 209 and embroider each dot in satin stitch. Change to 3 strands of ecru and embroider the head, using satin stitch. At this point, run a small line of stitches around the abdomen. Then fill in with long and short stitch, sewing around the dots and over your guide stitches. Once completed, use a single strand of ecru and sew each leg and the antennae, securing them into the abdomen as you do so by sewing them in.

Wash and iron.

Lavender & dragonfly continental pillowcase

The lavender-and-dragonfly theme used on the duvet cover can be carried over onto other items of bed-linen with slight variations. Here I used a very simple design of three single lavender sprigs, with a single dragonfly. This design is also suitable for cushions, laundry-bags, curtains, and so on. Instead of a dragonfly, you could use a bee, a ladybird or even a combination of all three.

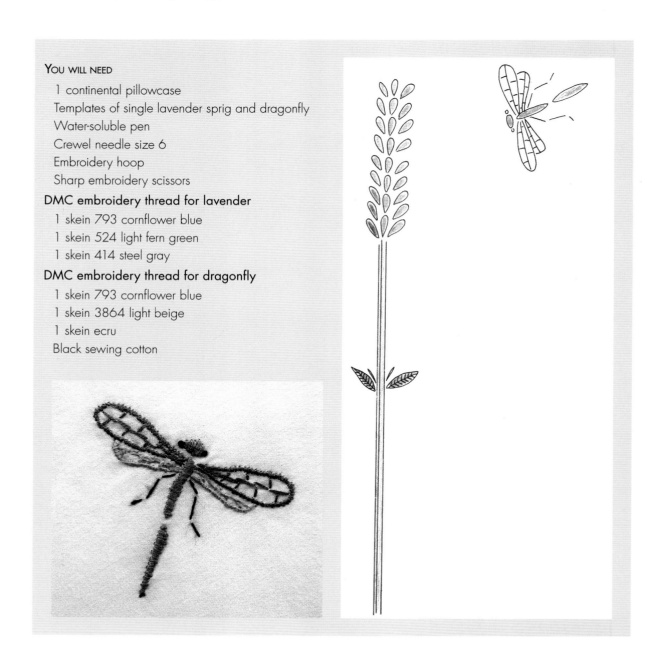

YOU WILL NEED

1 continental pillowcase
Templates of single lavender sprig and dragonfly
Water-soluble pen
Crewel needle size 6
Embroidery hoop
Sharp embroidery scissors

DMC embroidery thread for lavender

1 skein 793 cornflower blue
1 skein 524 light fern green
1 skein 414 steel gray

DMC embroidery thread for dragonfly

1 skein 793 cornflower blue
1 skein 3864 light beige
1 skein ecru
Black sewing cotton

Lay out the pillowcase on a flat surface. Using a water-soluble pen, mark on it where the sprigs should be placed. Fold the pillowcase in half vertically and in half again, pressing along each fold line. Unfold, and place a sprig on each crease line.

Transfer the design by tracing it through the pillowcase, drawing it on freehand, or using carbon-paper (see page 10). At the same time trace the dragonfly, as if it is flying towards one of the sprigs.

Embroider the lavender stem in stem stitch, using 3 strands of DMC 524. When you reach a leaf, divert and sew the leaf in fishbone stitch. Once you have completed the stem in DMC 524, change to DMC 414 and sew another line of stem stitch against

the left-hand side of the stem and along the bottom of the left leaf. This creates a shadow line and gives the stem some weight.

Embroider the petals in lazy daisy stitch, using 3 strands of DMC 793.

Now sew the dragonfly. Use 3 strands of DMC 793 and sew the abdomen in raised satin stitch. Using a single strand of black cotton, sew each leg in straight stitches, and the eyes as French knots. Change to 3 strands of DMC 3864 and embroider the top section of the wing in couched satin stitch, and the lacy inset of the wing in single stitches.

Repeat for the bottom half of the wing, using 3 strands of DMC ecru.

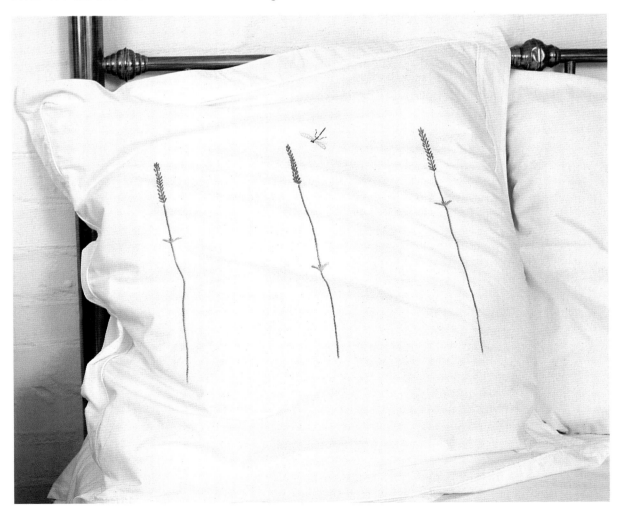

Lavender & dragonfly curtains

In the hot summer months I like to change my curtains to something light, floaty and airy that gives privacy, but does not block any cool breeze coming through open windows. With this in mind, I ordered two pairs of muslin tab-top curtains from a curtain manufacturer to fit my windows. They are also available ready-made, or you can easily make them yourself.

Since they were for my bedroom, I continued the lavender and dragonfly theme, embroidering the designs onto voile rectangles which I machine-stitched onto the curtains. You could also embroider the design straight onto the curtain muslin, but I rather liked the mix of the two sheer fabrics. As a nice touch, you could leave the top of one lavender square open, creating a pocket, and put dried lavender heads into it, or perhaps single sprigs of lavender, so that the smell wafts into the room with the breeze.

You will need

1 pair of muslin curtains to fit your window
0,25 m (10 in) voile (this is ample for 8 squares)
Templates of lavender and dragonfly
Water-soluble pen and ruler
Crewel needle size 6
Embroidery hoop
Sewing machine
White sewing cotton
Scissors
Sharp embroidery scissors

DMC embroidery thread in the following colours

1 skein 524 light fern green
1 skein 3817 light celadon green
1 skein 793 cornflower blue
1 skein 414 steel gray or 524 light fern green
1 skein 340 blue violet
Black sewing cotton

First decide how many squares you want on your curtains. I placed 4 rectangles 12 x 15 cm (4¾ x 6 in) equidistantly on the leading edge of each curtain. Measure out rectangles on the voile and trace the designs onto the squares (see page 10).

Voile is quite tricky to draw on because it moves. It helps to have someone hold the material for you as you draw.

Embroider the lavender. Place the fabric into your embroidery hoop and use 3 strands of 524 thread to embroider each lavender stem in stem stitch. Change to 3 strands of cornflower blue thread to embroider each lavender petal in lazy daisy stitch.

Embroider the dragonfly a little differently from the one on the duvet cover to allow for the sheer fabric.

Begin by working the legs first, in couched satin stitch, using 1 length of ordinary black cotton. To do this effectively on the voile, I first made single straight stitches along each section of leg and then stitched over in satin stitch. The loose strands will be stitched in when you work the body.

Change to 3 strands of DMC 793 and work the head and body in couched satin stitch.

Change to 3 strands of DMC 3817 and work each eye as a French knot. Using 1 strand of black cotton, add a smaller French knot on top of the green.

Using 3 strands of the same green thread, work the top wings in couching stitch and the lacy inset in straight stitch. Change to 3 strands of DMC 524 and stitch the bottom half of the wing in couched satin stitch and the lacy inset in straight stitch

Once completed, rinse off any pen marks and allow to dry. Carefully cut out the voile rectangles, then pin and tack hems all round. Pin and tack the rectangles into position on the curtain and machine stitch.

If you wish to make a pocket for sprigs of lavender, double-hem the top edge, then machine-stitch the other three sides onto the curtain.

You can use Fraystop (see page 35) on voile to help stiffen the edges and to prevent fraying.

Lavender and petals for the bathroom

I continued the main bedroom's lavender theme for the bathroom to individualise a waffle hand-towel. The bee is added for a bit of fun. You could also use a ladybird, dragonfly or all three bugs. The simple petal and leaf design used on the bath towel and bath mat is one of my favourites. It's simple and effective and changes a plain towel into something unique. You can use a single colour as I have done here, or embroider the petals and leaves in complementary colours to suit your colour scheme. Choose a towel with a plain border and draw the design onto this.

You will need

- 1 waffle-cotton hand-towel
- 1 bath towel
- 1 cotton bath rug
- Templates of lavender, bee and petals
- Water-soluble pen
- Tape-measure
- Crewel needle size 6
- Embroidery hoop
- Sharp embroidery scissors

DMC embroidery thread in the following colours

- 1 skein 3817 celadon green
- 1 skein 793 cornflower blue
- 1 skein 725 topaz (yellow)
- 1 skein 310 black
- 1 skein 3864 light beige
- 1 skein ecru
- 1 skein tapestry wool in ecru

Lay the **hand-towel** out and transfer the design as described on page 10. Place the towel in your embroidery hoop.

For the lavender, use 3 strands of green to work the stem in stem stitch. As you reach each leaf, divert and work in fishbone stitch. Change to 3 strands of blue and work each petal in lazy daisy stitch.

Work the bee, using 3 strands of black thread to stitch the antennae as two small straight stitches. Now work the head and body stripes in satin stitch. Stitch the wings with 3 strands of DMC 3864 in fishbone stitch. Change to 3 strands of yellow and work the remaining stripes in satin stitch, sewing in any loose threads. Once completed, wash to remove pen marks.

If you wish, add a variety of bugs all over the towel, flying into the lavender.

As you work, make sure the back of the work is kept neat by sewing in any loose threads, or tidy up afterwards.

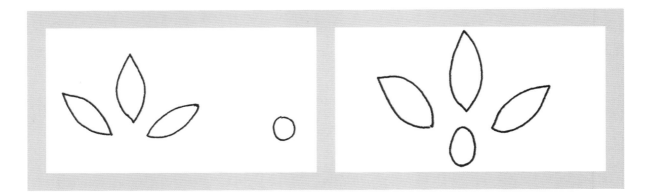

Lay out the **towel** and transfer the design. Use your tape-measure to ensure the space between the motifs is the same. Place the towel in the embroidery hoop.

Use 3 strands of DMC ecru to stitch each leaf and petal in raised satin stitch. Work a single dot in between motifs in the same way. Wash to remove any pen marks.

Transfer the design to the border of the **bathmat**, measuring carefully with your tape measure to ensure the motifs are equally spaced. Place the rug in the embroidery hoop. Use 1 length of wool (yes, it will go through the eye of the needle) to stitch each petal in satin stitch, following your pen marks. Work the dot in satin stitch. Rinse to remove any pen marks.

Camomile & bee guest-towel

Herbs make a wonderful subject for embroidery. This camomile design has been stitched onto a textured cotton guest-towel. The bees add a pretty touch, as well as being fun. This design could look equally effective on almost anything from serviettes to bed-linen.

YOU WILL NEED

1 small guest-towel
Template of camomile and bee
Water-soluble pen
Tape-measure
Crewel needle size 6
Embroidery hoop
Sharp embroidery scissors

DMC embroidery thread in the following colours

1 skein 725 topaz (yellow)
1 skein ecru
1 skein 3347 yellow green
1 skein 310 black

Lay out the **towel** and transfer the design of the camomile as described on page 10. Once the camomile is in position, draw bees flying in from the top. Scatter them over the material, but let them all face downwards towards the camomile.

Place the towel in your embroidery hoop and work the stem in stem stitch, using 3 strands of green. As you reach each leaf, divert and work as a single straight stitch. Change to 3 strands of ecru and work the petals in lazy daisy stitch. Now work the centres of the camomile as French knots, using 3 strands of yellow.

Work the bee, using 3 strands of black to stitch the head and the body stripes in satin stitch. Now stitch the wings in lazy-daisy stitch, using 3 strands of ecru. For a more textured look, use fishbone stitch.

Change to 3 strands of yellow and work the remaining stripes in satin stitch, sewing in any loose threads.

Once completed, wash to remove pen marks.

My friend, Jane, says this reminds her of Winnie-the-Pooh! I think it's all the bees.

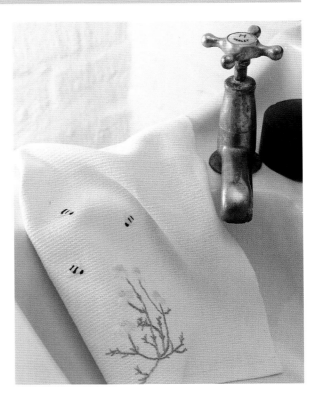

Simple daisies on a pillowcase

This simple design turns an ordinary pillowcase into something special. The flowers are worked in lazy daisy stitch, with a single yellow stitch at the top of the petal, which repeats the colour used at the centre of the daisy. For extra effect, a border in chevron stitch has been worked across the pillowcase.

You can match the colours to an existing colour scheme, or even use a variety of colours for a riotous effect! This design would also look effective stitched along the edge of a flat sheet, with two borders of chevron stitch and daisies in between.

If you are embroidering a pair of pillowcases for a double bed, it will look most effective with the embroidered edge on the short outside edges. When drawing on the design, draw both pillowcases at the same time to make sure they lie correctly.

YOU WILL NEED

1 pillowcase
Template of daisy
Water-soluble pen
Crewel needle size 6
Ruler
Embroidery hoop
Sharp embroidery scissors

DMC embroidery thread in the following colours
1 skein 340 blue violet
1 skein 725 topaz (yellow)

Lay out the pillowcase and using a ruler and water-soluble pen, mark how far from the edge you want the border to be. Carefully draw two straight lines 1 cm apart. These are the top and bottom guides for the chevron stitch.

Draw the daisy design in the space between these lines and the edge of the pillowcase, using the water-soluble pen and daisy template. Scatter the daisies randomly or place them in rows. I usually embroider the daisies first, but it is up to you where you start.

Place the pillowcase in your embroidery hoop framing one daisy design. Using 3 strands of yellow, stitch the centre in satin stitch. Change to 3 strands of violet blue and work each petal in a lazy daisy stitch.

Now use 3 strands of yellow again and work a single stitch over the top of the lazy daisy stitch.

Work the border in chevron stitch, using 3 strands of violet blue. Once completed, wash off any pen marks and iron it.

This has since become one of my favourite designs, and I have had great fun using different colour combinations for the daisies and the border.

Play around with lovely bright colours and see how effective it looks.

Voile café curtain with daisies

Sheer fabric has become very popular for using around the home. In this project I have used voile to make a café-style curtain that has a simple daisy-type design embroidered onto it. Although I have used blue and green for my colour choice, this design would look beautiful worked in either white or cream thread as a subtle contrast to the sheer material.

Do not be daunted by the delicate look of the fabric. It is a little tricky to work on and because of its sheer nature all the sewing has to be neat, no loose ends. Personally I find that raised satin stitch works the best.

If you require a little more privacy at your window, muslin could be used instead of voile.

You will need

Length of voile, 1½ times width of your window
Template of daisy
Water-soluble pen
Tape-measure
Crewel needle size 6
Embroidery hoop
Sewing machine
White cotton for sewing
Scissors
Sharp embroidery scissors

DMC embroidery thread in the following colours

1 skein 906 parrot green
1 skein 793 cornflower blue

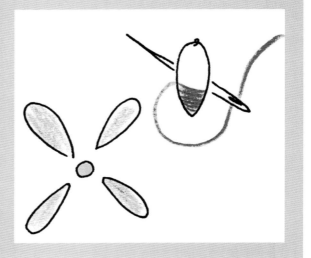

Because of the sheer, silky nature of this fabric, it does tend to move when one is drawing on it. Enlist some help to hold the fabric still or else secure the edges with masking tape. This is more important if the design is to be precisely placed. If one is scattering the design, a little movement won't matter so much.

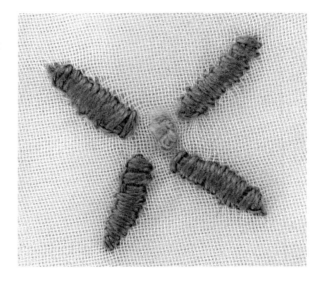

Lay out your fabric, mark where the daisies are to be placed with a water-soluble pen and transfer the design (see page 10). Although I have scattered the daisies over the fabric, the curtain will look equally effective with the daisies placed in a row along the bottom edge or even around all four edges of the curtain. Place the fabric in your embroidery hoop. Try to get it as taut as possible in the hoop by tightening the screw on the side. (You may need a screwdriver for this, although I can do mine by hand.) I alternated the colours of the petals and the centre for each daisy.

Using 3 strands of thread, work the centre dot in satin stitch. Make sure that all the ends are sewn in. Now change to your petal colour and using 3 strands of thread, make a lazy daisy stitch for each petal. Over-sew each lazy daisy stitch in small satin stitches. Make sure all ends are sewn in.

Repeat for the remaining daisies, alternating the colours if you wish.

Once the embroidery is done, machine-stitch hems in the sides of the curtain. I used small zigzag stitches for a neat finish on the sheer fabric. Fold over 8 cm (3¼ in) at the top. Stitch a tube wide enough for your curtain hooks and wire or dowel to go through.

Don't do what I did and make the whole curtain and then realise that the tube actually wasn't wide enough for the dowel to go through. Oh well, what is it they say about mistakes being a valuable part of life?

Tractor duvet-cover & pillowcase

Tractors are my son David's great love in life. In fact his first word was *tractor*! So, with that in mind I designed him his own tractor duvet, based on a drawing by my seven-year-old daughter. The theme expanded to a farmyard and I had a lot of fun using a mixture of appliqué and embroidery to make up the various elements, which include cows, sheep, pigs, boys and girls, houses and trees.

To complement the tractor duvet cover, I added a pillowcase in green gingham to match the treetops on the duvet cover. I decorated the pillowcase with three blocks of white cotton onto which more tractors have been embroidered.

You can also stitch a panel with various motifs and sew this onto a gingham cushion or across the bottom of a plain roman blind. Or use individual motifs to decorate laundry-bags or a small cushion.

You will need

Plain single duvet-cover (white or colour of choice)
Scraps of fabric for appliqué
0,75 m (29 in) lime green gingham for pillowcase
1 m white cotton for pillowcase backing & patches
Farmyard templates
Water-soluble pen and ruler
Crewel needle size 6
Embroidery hoop
Scissors
Zig-zag scissors for cutting out appliqué
Sewing cotton
Sewing machine
DMC embroidery thread in bright colours matching the fabric you are using for appliqué

DMC thread for cows, pigs, sheep, dog, horse

310 black
Ecru
957 pale geranium
353 peach
414 steel gray
Ecru tapestry wool
838 dark beige brown
3864 light beige

For children

310 black
907 light parrot green
793 cornflower blue
921 copper
725 topaz (yellow)

For cars, grass, tractors, flowers, bugs

Ecru
666 bright red
310 black
725 topaz (yellow)
792 dark cornflower blue
793 cornflower blue
906 parrot green
910 emerald green
971 pumpkin

The number of skeins needed depends on the number of motifs you are going to sew. For this single duvet and pillowcase I used 1 skein each of all colours, except black and ecru, of which I used 2 skeins each.

Transfer the design to the duvet. Lay out the duvet and mark the positions where the motifs are to be placed, using the water-soluble pen. This project has 5 rows of motifs, alternately spaced across the cover.

Working from the top, the first row is placed 55 cm (21½ in) from the top of the duvet and 51 cm (20 in) from the right-hand edge. The second row starts 32 cm (12½ in) from the left and 73 cm (28¾ in) from the top. The third row starts 63 cm (24¾ in) from the right-hand side and 102 cm (40 in) from the top. The fourth row starts 26 cm (10 in) from the left and 122 cm (48 in) from the top. The fifth row starts 52 cm (20½ in) from the right and 55 cm (21½ in) from the bottom of the duvet.

Use your water-soluble pen and ruler to draw straight lines, on which the characters are to stand.

Transfer the designs as described on page 10. Decide what fabric you will use for appliqué and draw the relevant shapes. Cut them out and put aside until you are ready to sew them in position.

First row: girl with plaits and dungarees, boy with blond hair and dungarees, horse, house, sunflower with butterfly, sports car, tree, grass between motifs.

Second row: two pigs, boy with ginger hair and fork, pick-up truck or bakkie, grass with yellow flowers in French knots in between.

Third row: grass, tree, two sheep, girl in dress, flowers and bumblebee, dog.

Fourth row: grass, tractor, two cows, flowers and bumblebee.

Fifth row: car, tree, house, tractor, grass with red flowers in French knots in between.

For the tractor, using 3 strands of black, stitch the wheels in satin stitch on duvet cover itself. Use the water-soluble pen to draw the shape of the tractor on your chosen fabric for applique. To appliqué, cut out the tractor shape with zig-zag scissors and pin in position on the duvet cover. Place in your embroidery hoop and sew on, using satin stitch and keeping the stitches small

and evenly spaced. To embroider the tractor body, use 3 strands of your chosen colour and fill in with long and short stitch. Change to 3 strands of black and embroider the steering wheel and seat in single straight stitch.

For the bubble car, begin by stitching the tyres in satin stitch, using 3 strands of thread. Stitch the exhaust and steering wheel in small straight stitches. Change to 3 strands of green and stitch around the roof of the car in satin stitch. Use the same colour to stitch the body of the car in long and short stitch.

Do the **sports car** as you did the bubble car, but without a roof.

For the pick-up truck or bakkie, stitch the tyres as for car, tractor and sports car. Stitch the cab, using 3 strands of your chosen colour, in long and short stitch. Stitch around the roof in satin stitch. Use your water-soluble pen to draw a rectangle for the back section of the truck on your chosen fabric. Cut out, pin and appliqué in position.

For the tree, use 3 strands of brown and work the trunk in satin stitch. Using your water-soluble pen, draw the tree-shape onto green gingham or other chosen fabric. Cut out, pin and appliqué in position, using 3 strands of green.

The house is worked using appliqué only. Lay out your chosen fabric and, using the water-soluble pen, draw a square for the house and triangle for the roof onto the fabric. Cut out and pin in position. Stitch onto the duvet, using small, even and closely spaced stitches. (You can use a contrasting colour thread to stitch around the house and roof, and use a different fabric for the roof.) Sew the windows and doors in straight stitch. Stitch two squares for the windows and a rectangle for the door. Add a French knot as a doorknob.

For the sunflower, using 3 strands of DMC 906 green, work the stem in stem stitch. Change to 3 strands of DMC 725 yellow and sew the petals in lazy daisy stitch. Use 3 strands of DMC 971 pumpkin and work the centre of the sunflower as French knots.

For the bees, stitch the black stripes in satin stitch, using 3 strands of black thread. Change to DMC 725 and work the yellow stripes as satin stitch.

Change to 3 strands of ecru and work each wing as a lazy daisy stitch.

For the sheep, begin by using 3 strands of black and stitch two eyes, using French knots. Sew each ear in lazy daisy stitch. Sew each leg in a single stitch. Change to 3 strands of pink and stitch the nose in satin stitch. Now stitch the body and face, using all 6 strands of ecru in tightly spaced French knots. Take care not to sew over the eyes.

To make sure the legs are secure, work in the following way. Make a single straight stitch down the first leg, bringing the needle out at the back of the work. Now make a single stitch back up the same leg to the body of the sheep, bringing the needle out at the front of the work. Now move across to the second leg and repeat. Do this for all four legs. This ensures that each leg is secure. When you work the French knots on the body, make sure that any black stitches showing on the front of the work are covered.

The sheepdog is worked in the same way as the sheep, but for extra texture I used ecru tapestry wool instead of embroidery thread.

For the cow, using 3 strands of black, embroider each eye with a French knot. Using the same length of thread, move up and sew each ear as a single straight stitch. Work each black patch in satin stitch. The tail is worked using a single straight stitch, with tiny stitches on the end to look like hair. The legs are four straight stitches (see instructions for sheep).

Change to 3 strands of DMC 353 to sew the nose and udder. Work the nose and udder in satin stitch and add 2 straight stitches at the bottom of the udder for the teats. Now change to 3 strands of DMC ecru and fill in the face and body with long and short stitch, sewing around the eyes, nose and black patches.

For the pig, using 3 strands of black, work the eyes and hole in the snout as French knots. Change to DMC 957 and stitch the nose in satin stitch, taking care to stitch around the nostrils. Change to 3 strands of DMC 414 grey and work each ear as a lazy daisy stitch. Using the same colour, work each spot in satin stitch and each leg as a single straight stitch. Stitch the tail in couching stitch to get a curled look.

For the body and face, change to 3 strands of DMC 353 peach. Work the face in satin stitch. Start from the bottom of the face and sew from the snout outwards, keeping each stitch horizontal. As you work towards the top of the head, begin to make each stitch more vertical, stitching around the eyes. Work the body in long and short stitch, stitching around the grey patches.

Sew the horse by using 3 strands of black and stitching 2 French knots as eyes. Work the nostrils in satin stitch, using 3 strands of DMC 353 peach. Change to 3 strands of DMC 3864 and work the face in satin stitch. Work around the nostrils and eyes. Sew each ear as lazy daisy stitch. Work the body and legs in long and short stitch.

To work the forelock, use 3 strands of DMC 838 and stitch four loops roughly 1 cm in length, securing them at the top with small single stitches. Snip through the bottom of the loop with your embroidery scissors. This gives a "hair" effect that works quite nicely.

Work the tail and forelock in the same way, but make the loops longer for the tail, securing them in the same place on the horse's back. Make the loops for the forelock shorter.

Work the children in a mixture of appliqué and stitching. I varied the hair by using French knots to simulate curls, and long and short stitch for straight hair.

For the girl with plaits and dungarees, using the template, draw the dungarees shape onto your chosen material. Cut out with zig-zag scissors. Pin in position and stitch on, using small even stitches in the colour of your choice. Add in a square pocket, using 3 straight stitches. For the face, change to 3 strands of black. Stitch each eye as a French knot. The nose is a single stitch. Work the mouth in couching stitch, ensuring the line curves upwards in a smile. Keep the couched stitches close together to create a solid line.

Still with black, work the fringe as straight stitches. The plaits are small cross stitches. Change to red and stitch 3 single stitches just above the end of the plaits to simulate hair ties. Still working in black, sew each arm in straight stitch. Sew the ends of the thread into the back of the work to make sure they are secure. Change to brown and sew the boots in satin stitch.

For the boy with blond hair and dungarees, using 3 strands of DMC 725 yellow, sew the blond hair in long and short stitch. Continue as for girl with dungarees.

Work the girl with dress as the previous 2 children, but use all 6 strands of black and work the hair in French knots. Sew the dress in satin stitch, using 3 strands of yellow for the top of the dress, and 3 strands of blue for the skirt and shoes. Work each leg as a single straight stitch in black.

Work the boy with ginger hair as other children. The clothes are sewn in satin stitch. The ginger hair is stitched in French knots, using all 6 strands of DMC 921. The fork is stitched in 3 strands of grey, using back stitch.

Fill in with grass, butterflies and flowers. Use 3 strands of green to make straight stitches along the bottom of the characters. Change to bright red and yellow and intersperse the grass with French knots to simulate wild flowers. To add in a small butterfly, stitch two single stitches in a V shape.

Stuff in a duvet, puff up a pillow and snuggle down with your son and make up farmyard stories.

For the pillowcase, using a water-soluble pen, draw 3 rectangles, each 6 x 8 cm (2 x 3 in) on the cotton. Trace the tractor motif in the centre of each rectangle.

Place the fabric in the embroidery hoop and begin by working the tyres in satin stitch, using 3 strands of black thread. Change to 3 strands of red and work one half of the tractor engine in satin stitch. Work the seat and steering wheel in straight stitch.

Change to 3 strands of DMC 792 dark cornflower blue and work the bottom half of the tractor engine in satin stitch. Make 2 straight stitches in the same colour for the funnel.

Add 2 French knots, using all six strands of ecru thread, to simulate smoke.

Add a single French knot in either red or DMC 792 in the centre of the back wheel, for the wheel hub.

Repeat this process for the other two tractors, changing colours to DMC 906 parrot green and blue, and DMC 725 topaz (yellow) and blue.

Once completed, wash to remove pen marks. Cut out the tractor rectangles. Lay out the green gingham and cut a rectangle 76 x 50 cm (30 x 20 in). Pin the embroidered rectangles in position, using a tape-measure to ensure the are equally spaced. Place the work in your embroidery hoop and stitch in position, using 3 strands of contrasting embroidery thread and working in satin stitch. Keep the stitches tight together and of an even size. For brightness I worked the top and bottom of each rectangle in a different colour to the sides. Repeat for all the embroidered rectangles.

When working with appliqué, use Fraystop, a liquid applied to the edges of the fabric to stop them from fraying. You will find it at most haberdashery shops.

Make the pillowcase. Lay out the material you are using for the back of the pillowcase and cut out two rectangles, one 50 by 40 cm (20 x 16 in) and the other 50 by 60 cm (20 x 24 in). Hem the 50 cm (20 (in) edge of each rectangle. With right sides facing, pin the 2 backing rectangles to the appliquéd front rectangle with the hemmed edges of the backing rectangles overlapping. Machine stitch together, finish the edges and trim the corners. Turn right side out and iron.

This is my son's favourite pillowcase and he will not go to sleep without it.

Ballerina duvet-cover

These fun and funky ballerinas are my daughter's favourite, and make a refreshing change from Barbies for a girl's bedroom. Make up a duvet-cover, using a plain white cotton sheet for the backing and chambray cotton cut to the exact same size for the top. The ballerinas are sewn onto white cotton patches, which are then machine-stitched in a line across the top of the duvet, with running stitches around the edge to add definition. The duvet cover I made up has a white border either side of the lilac mid-section. My lilac fabric wasn't wide enough, but I liked it, so I had to make a plan. For a reversible duvet cover, embroider the daisies used for the pillowcase (see page 39) onto the white cotton side.

YOU WILL NEED

1 single flat sheet in white cotton
Chambray cotton for front of duvet cut to same size
   as sheet (1,3 x 2,3 m (51 x 91 in) with 2 cm
   (1 in) seam allowance included)
White cotton for the ballerina patches and buttons
3 large flat buttons (2 cm (1 in) diameter)
Templates of ballerinas
Water-soluble pen
Tape-measure
Crewel needle size 6
Embroidery hoop
Sharp embroidery scissors
Sewing cotton
Sewing machine
Zig-zag scissors

DMC embroidery thread in the following colours:

1 skein 310 black
1 skein 725 topaz (yellow)
1 skein 340 blue violet
1 skein 3805 cyclamen pink
1 skein 957 pale geranium
1 skein 907 light parrot green
1 skein 5283 silver

Lay out the white cotton and use a water-soluble pen to mark out 3 patches, each 15 cm (6 in) square.

Transfer the ballerina designs to the cotton as described on page 10. Place the cotton in your embroidery hoop.

Sew ballerina with small crown. Using 3 strands of black, stitch each eye as a French knot. Work the nose as a single straight stitch and the mouth and chin in couched satin stitch.

Use all 6 strands of black to work the hair as a mass of French knots, leaving space for the crown.

Work the crown, using 3 strands of yellow mixed with 1 strand of silver. Use single straight stitches to follow the lines of the crown.

Now work the dress. Use 3 strands of violet blue and work around the outline of the dress in stem stitch.

Change to 3 strands of cyclamen pink and work the centre of the daisy on the bodice as a French knot and the petals as lazy daisy stitches. Using the same colour, work the triangles at the bottom of the skirt in satin stitch. Finish off by working a series of French knots on the skirt, using all 6 strands of DMC 725 yellow.

Change back to 3 strands of black and work each arm and leg in couched satin stitch. Keep the stitches

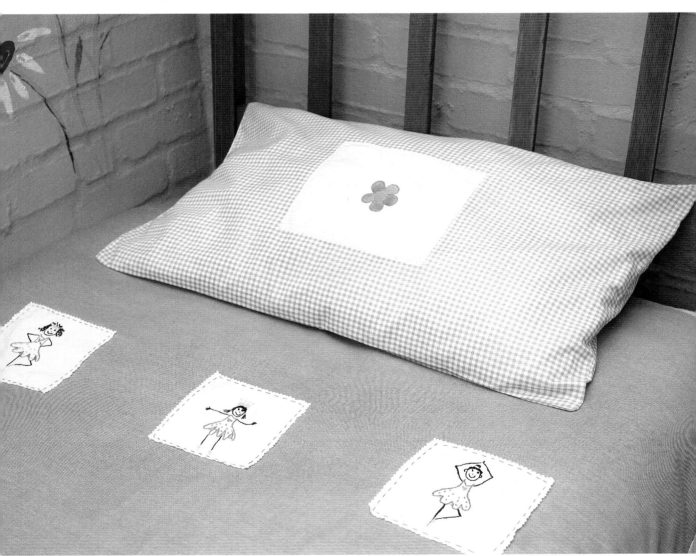

small and even. Finally, change to pale geranium and use 3 strands of thread to work each slipper in satin stitch.

Sew ballerina with big crown. Work the face as for ballerina with small crown. For the hair, use all 6 strands of black thread to work a series of French knots around the face. Then work 4 long straight stitches as the pigtail-ends. Stitch the hair-ties in satin stitch, using 3 strands of cyclamen pink.

Work the crown in 3 strands of yellow. You can also add a single strand of silver thread. Work the crown in satin stitch with a French knot above each point.

Using 3 strands of cyclamen pink, work the outline of the dress in stem stitch. Use 3 strands of blue violet thread to work the heart on the dress bodice in satin stitch. Finally change to 3 strands of green and work the skirt in French knots, and the triangles in between in satin stitch.

Change to 3 strands of black and work the arms in couched satin stitch. The fingers are worked with 5 straight stitches, varying the length of the fingers.

Work the legs using 3 strands of black and couched satin stitch, and the slippers using 3 strands of pale geranium and satin stitch.

Sew ballerina with bun. Work the face as for the other ballerinas. Use 3 strands of black and work the hair in satin stitch. Use 3 strands of yellow with 1 strand of silver thread to work the hair-band in satin stitch.

Using 3 strands of cyclamen pink, work the outline of the dress in stem stitch. Use 3 strands of green thread to work the heart on the dress bodice and the triangles at the bottom of the skirt in satin stitch.

Finally change to 3 strands of blue violet and work the skirt in French knots.

Change to 3 strands of black and work each arm and leg in couched satin stitch. Change to 3 strands of pale geranium and work each slipper in satin stitch.

Once the embroidery is completed, cut out the squares with zigzag scissors.

Make the duvet cover. Lay out the fabric you are using for the front and mark where you want to place the patches, using a tape measure to ensure they are equally spaced. Pin the squares in position and machine stitch. Use 3 strands of cyclamen pink and stitch a line of running stitches around the edge, over the line of machine stitches. I left the zig-zag edge for decoration.

Machine stitch a double hem in the bottom edge of the fabric. Place it on the white sheet, right sides facing, and machine stitch together, leaving an opening at the bottom large enough for a duvet to fit through.

Attach two sets of ribbons to close the opening. If you feel particularly creative, cover buttons with a simple embroidered design and close the opening with these, as I have done.

For the button embroidery, lay a button down on a scrap of white fabric and trace around it. Transfer the funky daisy design (see page 10) onto the fabric reducing it to fit. Embroider as described on page 39 and cut out with a 1,5 cm overlap. (Or draw a heart and embroider in long and short stitch). Machine-stitch a row of running stitch 5 mm from the edge. Lay the button down on the wrong side of the fabric and gather the running stitch so the fabric fits tightly around the button. Wind the gathering thread around the gathered edge and secure with satin stitch.

Hand-sew in position in the opening and make corresponding machine buttonholes.

As an alternative to ballerinas, if your daughter is into fairies, add wings to the designs. Work them the same way as the dragonfly wings on page 12. The ballerinas or fairies will also look funky stitched onto a T-shirt or sweatshirt.

Funky daisy pillowcase

To complement the ballerina duvet I embroidered this funky daisy onto a white cotton square and stitched it onto a lilac gingham pillowcase. I have also reduced the design and placed three motifs down the short edge of an ordinary white pillowcase and three down the centre of a scatter cushion. You could also embroider the daisies on the reverse side of the ballerina duvet for an interchangeable look for a girl's bedroom.

You will need

76 x 50 cm (30 x 20 in) lilac gingham
White cotton cut with pinking shears 50 x 60 cm
  (20 x 24 in), 50 x 40 cm (20 x 16 in) and
  20 x 20 cm (8 x 8 in)
Template of funky daisy design
Crewel needle size 6
Embroidery hoop
Sewing cotton & sewing machine
Sharp embroidery scissors

DMC emboidery thread in the following colours

1 skein 340 blue violet
1 skein 3805 cyclamen pink
1 skein 907 light parrot green

Transfer the design to the 20 x 20 cm (8 x 8 in) white cotton square as described on page 10. Place the fabric in the embroidery hoop.

Stitch the outline of the daisy using 3 strands of cyclamen pink and stem stitch. Change to 3 strands of violet blue and stitch the petals in long and short stitch. Now change to 3 strands of green and work the centre of the daisy in long and short stitch. Wash to remove any pen marks, allow to dry and iron.

Make the pillow case. Pin and tack the embroidered square to the centre of the gingham rectangle. Machine stitch in position.

Hem the 50 cm (20 in) edge of each white rectangle. With right sides facing and hemmed edges overlapping, pin the white rectangles to the appliquéd gingham

rectangle. Machine stitch together, finish the edges and trim the corners.

Turn right side out and press the seams.

Pop in a pillow and see how nice it looks on the bed combined with the ballerina duvet!

Personalized laundry-bag

Since my daughter Emma was getting new-look bed-linen, I decided to follow the theme through with a gingham laundry-bag with her name embroidered on it. I embroidered her name on white cotton, which I stitched onto the bag in lilac thread. Use the same letter templates and embroidery method for monogrammed serviettes or towels. It is deceptively simple and makes wonderful personalized gifts.

YOU WILL NEED

Two rectangles of lilac gingham, each 55 x 60 cm
   (21½ x 24 in), seam allowance included
1½ m (1 ¾ yd) cord for the drawstring
Sewing machine
White cotton patch for the name or initials, cut out
with pinking shears
Water-soluble pen
Ruler
Crewel needle size 6
Embroidery hoop
Sharp embroidery scissors
Sewing cotton
1-2 skeins DMC 210 lavender

Draw a straight line onto the white cotton using a water-soluble pen and ruler. This is the baseline for the letters. Mark the centre. Trace the letters you require onto the baseline, starting in the centre (for 'Emma' I started with the M's).

Place the fabric in your embroidery hoop. Use 3 strands of thread and work each letter in padded satin stitch. First sew a line of running stitches vertically along the outline of each letter.

Use several lines of stitches where the letter is wide. Sew over these lines in satin stitch. This gives a raised look to the work.

Make the draw-string bag. Pin and tack the embroidered patch to the front of one gingham rectangle and machine stitch.

Place gingham rectangles right sides together and machine stitch sides and bottom.

Fold over 1 cm (½ in) at the top edge and machine stitch. Fold over 10 cm (4 in) and press.

Form a casing by sewing two rows of stitches, one 7,5 cm (3 in) from the top and the second 9,5 cm (3 ¾ in) from the top. Turn right side out.

Carefully unpick seam stitching between the two rows of casing stitches. Cut the cord to roughly twice the width of the bag.

Attach a safety pin to one end and ease the cord through the casing.

Knot the two ends together and pull the cord to gather the top of the bag.

Now there is no excuse for Emma to leave dirty-clothes on the floor!

ABCDEFGHIJKLMNOP
QRSTUVWXYZ

Hot-air balloon cot-bumper

This is another example of the effective combination of embroidery and simple applique. To make it more tactile, I filled the balloon with a little stuffing. The basket is worked in a simple but effective basket stitch. Just for fun, add a small bird or birds flying around the balloon. Repeat the design in different colours on all three sections of the cot bumper.

Good themes for a nursery are farm animals, bugs, stars, hearts, daisies, ballerinas, sea creatures and boats. Match your theme to the nursery colour scheme with a mixture of embroidery and appliqué. Carry the theme through onto cushions, nappy-bags, nursery bags, panels for blinds or curtains, and even clothing. A nursery is the one place where you can let your imagination run riot!

You WILL NEED

1 ready-made cot-bumper (available from most baby shops with a removable foam inner)
Scraps of fabric for appliqué
Stuffing for the balloon
Template of hot-air balloon
Water-soluble pen
Tape-measure
Ruler
Crewel needle size 6
Embroidery hoop
Sharp embroidery scissors

DMC embroidery thread in the following colours

2 skeins ecru
1 skein 3864 light beige
1 skein 793 cornflower blue
1 skein 907 light parrot green
1 skein 310 black
1 skein 725 topaz (yellow)
1 skein 3750 dark antique blue
1 skein 304 medium red

Remove the foam inner of the cot-bumper. Lay out the cover and trace the design onto the centre of each section. Draw a heart in the centre of each fabric scrap to be used for the balloons.

Place the fabric in the emboidery hoop and work each heart in satin stitch, using three strands of red. Cut out the circles, 6 cm (2 ½ in) in diameter or to fit the size of your design. Use Fraystop (see page 35) on the edges if the fabric frays easily.

Frame one motif on the cot-bumper with your embroidery hoop and using 3 strands of blue, work the basket in basket filling stitch. Change to 3 strands of black and work the eyes of the teddy as French knots and the nose and mouth in straight stitch.

Work the face and body of the teddy as French knots, using 3 strands of ecru thread. Make sure you sew around the eyes, nose and mouth.

Change to 2 strands of dark blue and work the balloon strings in couching stitch.

Using 3 strands of red, sew the teddy's jersey in satin stitch. Pin the balloon in position backed by a little stuffing. Use 3 strands of cornflower blue and stitch in position with satin stitch.

For the bird, use 3 strands of DMC 725 yellow and work the beak and eye in satin stitch. Sew the body in satin stitch, using 3 strands of green, and use 3 strands of dark blue to sew each wing in lazy daisy stitch.

This design looks lovely repeated all around the cot-bumper in a variety of fabrics and colours, and will give your baby something to focus on and touch.

Teddy bear cot-duvet set

These cuddly teddies, inspired by one of my son's teddies, have been one of my best-selling designs. Three teddies are embroidered across the centre of a ready-made cot-duvet cover. The jerseys and balloon can be either embroidered, or appliquéd, giving you the ideal opportunity to repeat fabrics that may have been used elsewhere in the nursery.

The use of French knots for the fur makes the teddies very tactile and cuddly. The same theme can be carried through to cot bumpers, towels and even clothing.

The cot pillowcase has simply been decorated with an appliquéd heart.

YOU WILL NEED

1 ready-made cot-duvet cover set
Should you wish to make up your own,
  the size is 1,2 m x 82 cm (47¼ x 32¼ in),
  including seam allowances. The pillowcase
  is 40 x 34 cm (15½ x 13½ in)
Templates of teddies
Water-soluble pen
Tape-measure
Ruler
Crewel needle size 6
Embroidery hoop
Sharp embroidery scissors
Scraps of fabric for appliqué
Stuffing for the balloon

DMC embroidery thread in the following colours
  2 skeins ecru
  2 skeins 3864 light beige
  1 skein 792 dark cornflower blue
  1 skein 725 topaz (yellow)
  1 skein 907 light parrot green
  1 skein 310 black
  1 skein 304 medium red

Lay out the duvet, find the middle and draw a line using a water-soluble pen and ruler. This is the baseline on which the teddies will sit. Mark the centre of the line, as well as the centre of each half. Transfer the designs to these positions as described on page 10.

Work teddy with balloon. Use 3 strands of black and sew the eyes as French knots. Stitch the nose in satin stitch and the mouth in straight stitches.

Use 3 strands of beige and stitch the inside of each ear in satin stitch.

Change to 6 strands of ecru and work the head, body and legs as tightly spaced French knots, taking care not to sew over the face detail. Sew each paw as straight stitches, following the template lines.

Use 3 strands of yellow and work the jersey in horizontal long and short stitch for the body, and satin stitch for the arms and ribbing around the bottom.

Draw a balloon shape on a scrap of material. Draw a small red heart in the middle and use 3 strands of red thread to work it in satin stitch. Cut out the balloon and pin into position backed with a little stuffing. Use Fraystop (see page 35) on the edges if the fabric frays easily.

Using 3 strands of blue, stitch the string of the balloon in stem stitch and continue around the balloon in small satin stitches, securing the fabric to the duvet.

Work teddy sitting down. Work the face and body in the same way as the teddy with the balloon. Also stitch the bottom of each foot in beige satin stitch.

Use a water-soluble pen to draw the jersey shape onto a scrap of fabric and work a small red heart in the centre using 3 strands of thread and satin stitch. Cut out the jersey and pin it into position. Using 3 strands of thread in a matching or contrasting colour, sew the jersey on, using small tightly spaced satin stitch.

Work teddy with flowers. Work the face, body and jersey in the same way as the other teddies.

Use 3 strands of green to sew the stem in stem stitch. Work each leaf as a lazy daisy stitch. Use 3 strands of blue and work the blue petals in lazy daisy stitch and the centre of the yellow daisies as a blue French knot.

Use 3 strands of yellow and work the petals in lazy daisy stitch. Add a red French knot at the centre of the blue daisies. Work the yellow bud in satin stitch.

Rinse off any pen marks and iron. For this design it is best to iron carefully on the wrong side to avoid flattening the French knots.

Decorate the pillowcase. Draw and cut out a heart from a piece of scrap fabric. Pin and tack this in position on the pillowcase.

Use 3 strands of DMC thread in a matching or contrasting colour and sew on the heart, using tightly spaced and even satin stitches.

Sea-life towel

These brightly coloured sea-creatures have been a consistent favourite. Here I embroidered them onto white cotton, machine-appliquéd these patches onto blue gingham and finally appliquéd the ginham blocks onto a cream towel. This is a lovely theme for children's bedrooms and bathrooms and can be used on bed-linen, curtains or blinds, cushions and drawstring bags, as well as on towels and face-cloths.

YOU WILL NEED

Towel
White cotton (3 x 10 cm (4 in) square)
Gingham (3 x 12 cm (5 in) square)
Templates of sea-life
Tape-measure
Water-soluble pen
Crewel needle size 6
Embroidery hoop
Sharp embroidery scissors

DMC embroidery thread in the following colours

1 skein 666 bright red
1 skein 312 dark baby blue
1 skein ecru
1 skein 906 parrot green

Transfer the designs onto the white cotton squares as described on page 10.

Sew the seahorse. Place the cotton in your embroidery hoop and using 3 strands of DMC 312 blue, work the eye and bubbles as French knots.

Change to 3 strands of DMC 666 red and work the sea-horse in satin stitch, starting from the top and sewing around the eye. When you reach the tail, curve the stitches around the curl.

Sew the whale. Use 3 strands of ecru to work the mouth, gills and plume in straight stitch. Sew the eye as a French knot and the one fin in satin stitch. Work the body, using 3 strands of DMC 312 blue and long and short stitch, sewing around the mouth, gills and detail.

Sew the starfish. I placed a single green French knot at the centre, but if you do not have this colour, use the blue. (It's unnecessary to buy a skein of green for a single French knot.)

Change to 3 strands of red and work each leg section in satin stitch, leaving an opening at the centre (see the template).

Once completed, wash the cotton to remove any carbon or pen marks. Allow to dry, press and machine stitch the embroidery pieces to the gingham squares using satin stitch (or sew the embroidery on by hand, using satin stitch).

Finally, machine stitch these gingham patches onto the towel, spacing them equally.

My children are already fighting over whose towel this is!

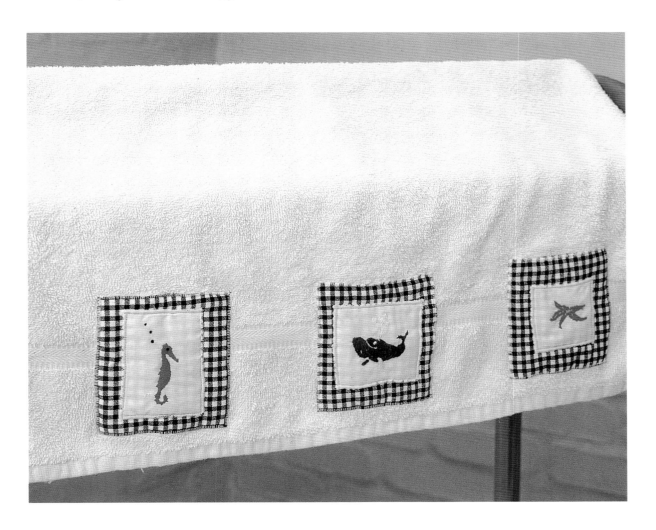

Boots on towels or pillowcases

The inspiration for these boats caused me to crash my car twice! While driving above Kalk Bay harbour I spied a classic tugboat heading out to sea. I had to sketch it and scratched around for a pen and piece of paper while waiting for the traffic light to change. Meanwhile, my foot had come of the brake, the car rolled forward and I banged into the car in front of me. I pulled over and jumped out red-faced to apologise and check for damage. While exchanging details with the owner of the bashed car, to my horror, my car rolled past me and bashed into her car again! I rushed back to my car, leapt in to pull up my handbrake and was even more red-faced as my victim remarked, "You're not having a very good day, are you". But I got my sketch and here it is, with other boats in a mixture of appliqué and embroidery in a simple folk-art style.

YOU WILL NEED

1 pillowcase
Scraps of fabric for the appliqué (I used blue gingham with red thread to create a nautical feel)
Templates of boats
Tape-measure
Water-soluble pen

Crewel needle size 6
Embroidery hoop
Sharp embroidery scissors
DMC embroidery thread in the following colours
1 skein 321 red
1 skein 791 dark cornflower blue

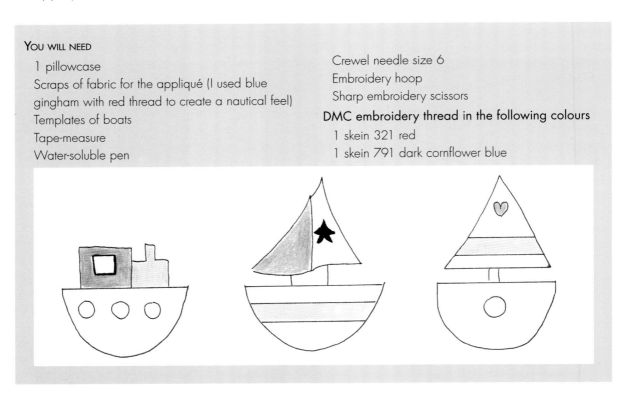

Lay out the pillowcase and draw a straight line across the middle with a water-soluble pen. Trace or copy the designs onto the line, spaced equally.

Work the tugboat. Using 3 strands of blue, stitch around the outline of the boat in stem stitch. Cut out the fabric for the funnel bottom to be appliquéd and stitch this on, using small even satin stitches. I used 3 strands of DMC 791 blue to complement the colour of the fabric.

Work the top of the funnel in satin stitch, using the same thread.

Change to 3 strands of red and work the cabin in satin stitch, sewing around the window. Still using 3 strands of red, work each porthole in couching stitch.

Work yacht with two sails. Use 3 strands of red and work the bottom of the boat in satin stitch.

Change to 3 strands of blue and work the top section of the boat in satin stitch. Fill in the outline between the red and blue bands in stem stitch.

Work the round porthole in couching stitch, also using 3 strands of blue thread. Each mast is worked as a single stitch with 3 strands of blue thread.

Cut out the sail to be appliquéd and stitch it on, using satin stitch and 3 strands of matching thread.

Change to 3 strands of red and work the outline of the other sail in stem stitch, finishing off by sewing the star in satin stitch.

Work yacht with one sail. Cut out the boat shape from your scrap fabric. Use 3 strands of matching thread to stitch it on, using satin stitch. Work the mast in satin stitch.

Cut the middle section of the sail from scrap fabric and stitch on along the top and two sides, using satin stitch. Work the outline of the sail in stem stitch.

Change to 3 strands of red and work the bottom section of the sail in satin stitch, sewing over the bottom edge of the fabric section.

Finally, work the heart and porthole in satin stitch, still using 3 strands of red.

To finish off the design, work a line of running stitches in waves beneath the boats. Alternatively, hand-write a nautical message such as bon voyage and work this in running stitches.

If you do see inspiration while driving around, please park first and make sure your handbrake is on!

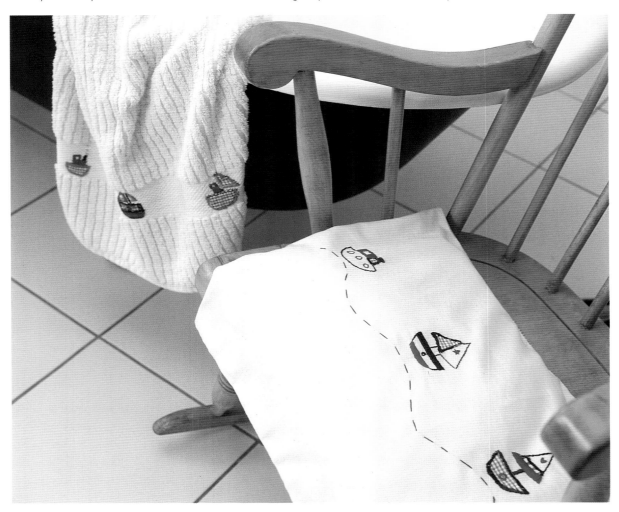

Cockerel on a tablecloth

This design was inspired by a plate from Portugal. The colours are bright, reminiscent of long, hot days in the sun. A simple border, picking up the colours in the cockerel, finishes off the tablecloth beautifully. The same design could work equally well reduced in size and stitched onto serviettes, tea-towels, aprons, tea-cosies, and so on. I added orange, red and green ready-made serviettes with the border daisy stitched in one corner.

The tablecloth itself is a single cotton sheet that I picked up during one of my junk shop rummages. A hot wash and iron with spray starch and it was as good as new.

<table>
<tr><td>

You will need

1 white cotton sheet or ready-made tablecloth
6 serviettes (optional, see page 53)
Templates of cockerels and border design
Water-soluble pen
Crewel needle size 6
Embroidery hoop
Tape-measure and ruler

</td><td>

DMC embroidery thread in the following colours

1 skein 304 medium red
1 skein 310 black
4 skeins 791 dark cornflower blue
2 skeins 907 light parrot green
4 skeins 725 topaz (yellow)
1 skein 971 pumpkin (orange)
   or 1 skein 721 medium orange spice

</td></tr>
</table>

Transfer the design as described on page 10 after having carefully marked the centre (for the cockerel) and the positions for the border motifs. I spaced mine at 20 cm (8 in) intervals. It helps to draw this border with the cloth on the table where it will be used, so that you can see exactly where the border should go.

Embroider the cockerel. Using 3 strands of DMC 310 black, work the eye in satin stitch. Work the black lines on the body and the legs in couched satin stitch. Make sure you stick to the curve of the legs as you sew. Change to 3 strands of DMC 971 pumpkin orange and work the beak in satin stitch. The line around the neck is worked with the same thread in stem stitch. Work the area in front of the tail feathers in long and short stitch. As you work the body of the cockerel, lay the stitches in the direction the feathers would normally lie. Stitch around the black and catch any loose black threads underneath the orange and as you sew.

Change to 3 strands of DMC 725 yellow and work the head and main body in long and short stitch. Take care not to pull the tablecloth too tightly in your embroidery hoop, which may stretch your fabric.

Change to 3 strands of DMC 304 red and work the plumes on top of the head as well as the crop in long and short stitch.

Finally, work the tail with 3 strands of DMC 791 blue in long and short stitch. Curve the stitches in the direction of the tail feathers as you work.

Work the border, alternating between blue, green and yellow. The dots are worked using 3 strands of thread in satin stitch. The petals are also worked with 3 strands of thread, but in long and short stitch.

When working large areas in long and short stitch, release the tension slightly in your embroidery hoop. This prevents the fabric, onto which you are working, from pulling.

Bugs & flowers on serviettes

Serviettes are easy to decorate with embroidery and make lovely gifts. You can use just about any design in a corner, or decorate the entire border. When working serviettes, take care that the design is not placed too close to the edge or you will not be able to fit it in the embroidery hoop. I know this from experience!

Keeping the back as neat as the front is particularly important when you are stitching a serviette, so check both sides as you work and make sure that any loose threads are sewn in (see Starting and finising off, page 10). Try these designs: a gecko (also lovely on a hand-towel), melon and bug, cabbage and ladybird or a single daisy.

YOU WILL NEED

Serviettes, ready-made, or fabric to sew your own
Template of designs
Water-soluble pen or dressmaker's carbon paper
Crewel needle size 6
Embroidery hoop
Small sharp embroidery scissors

DMC embroidery thread for gecko

1 skein 906 parrot green
1 skein 310 black
1 skein 904 dark green

For melon and bug

1 skein 906 parrot green
1 skein 310 black or black sewing cotton
1 skein ecru
1 skein 352 light coral
1 skein 677 light old gold

For brightly-coloured daisy

1 skein 906 parrot green
1 skein 725 topaz (yellow)
1 skein 606 bright orange-red

For cabbage and ladybird

1 skein Coton Perlé no 5 mid-green
1 skein ecru
1 skein 3348 light green
1 skein 934 black avocado green
1 skein 666 bright red
Black sewing cotton

Embroider the serviettes. If you decided to add serviettes to the tablecloth, transfer the border daisy design, (see page 50) to the corner of each serviette and embroider in the same way as the border design using colours of your choice (see page 51).

Embroider the melon and bug. Lay out the serviette and transfer the design onto the corner of the serviette as described on page 10. Place the serviette in your embroidery hoop.

Using 3 strands of DMC 906 green, work the melon skin in satin stitch.

Change to 3 strands of ecru and work the pith in satin stitch. Now work each pip in satin stitch, using 3 strands of DMC 677. Finally change to 3 strands of DMC 352 and work the flesh in long and short stitch, sewing around the pips.

Use 3 strands of black and work the bug's head in satin stitch. Work each leg as a single straight stitch in the same colour. For a finer look, use just 1 strand or ordinary black sewing cotton for the legs.

Change to 3 strands of DMC 906 green and work the body of the bug in satin stitch. As you work the body, sew in any loose stitches from the legs.

Embroider the daisy. Lay out the serviette and transfer the daisy design onto one corner as described on page 10. Place the serviette in your embroidery hoop.

Use 3 strands of DMC 906 green and embroider the stem in stem stitch. Change to 3 strands of DMC 606 orange-red and work the centre of the daisy in satin stitch. Finally work each petal in couched satin stitch using 3 strands of DMC 725 yellow.

Embroider the cabbage and ladybird. Lay out the serviette and transfer the designs onto one corner as described on page 10. Place the serviette in your embroidery hoop.

Using 3 strands of ecru, work the white cabbage veins in straight stitch. Change to 3 strands of DMC 934 dark green and work the dark-shaded areas in satin stitch. Use 3 strands of DMC 3348 light green and work the centre of the cabbage in satin stitch.

Finally, fill in with 1 strand of mid-green perlé thread in satin stitch, working in sections, and around the veins and shading.

Work the ladybird in the same way as the bug, but use DMC 666 bright red for the body instead of green, and add black dots in satin stitch.

Wash the serviettes to remove pen and carbon marks, and iron carefully.

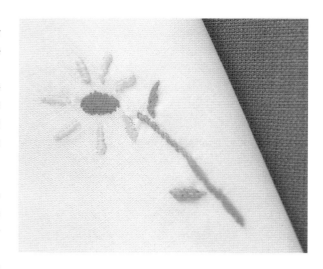

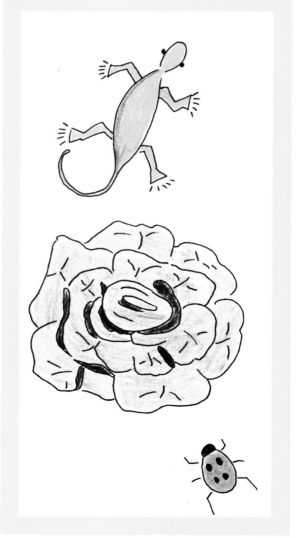

Embroider the gecko. Transfer the design to the corner of the serviette as described on page 10, adjusting the size as required.

Place the serviette in your embroidery hoop. Using 2 strands of DMC 310 black thread sew the toes of each foot in straight stitch.

Work an equal number of toes on the back and front of the serviette, and leave a length of thread to be sewn into the leg.

Change to 3 strands of black thread and sew each eye using French knots. Also sew eyes over on the back of the serviette.

Use 3 strands of brilliant green and sew the body, legs and tail in raised satin stitch, ensuring that any loose black threads are sewn in and hidden. Keep your stitches close together, especially on the tail section.

Work the side of the abdomen with 3 strands of dark green in satin stitch weaving into the main body

Felicia daisy tablecloth

I often find inspiration from the colours and shapes found in nature. The design on this tablecloth came from the felicia daisies growing in my garden. The blue of the petals is repeated in the mitred border, which also helps to add weight to the cloth. Mitring seems complicated, but is actually quite simple and gives your work a professional finish.

Use the table coth as an overlay on the diningroom table or on a small round or square table on the patio.

You will need

- Square piece of fabric in size of your choice
- Contrasting fabric for the border
- Template of felicia daisies
- Water-soluble pen
- Crewel needle size 6
- Embroidery hoop
- Sharp scissors
- Sewing cotton
- Protractor or other mathematical instrument set-square to draw a 45-degree line
- Sewing machine

DMC embroidery thread in the following colours

- 2 skeins 794 light cornflower blue
- 1 skein 725 topaz (yellow)
- 2 skeins 937 medium avocado green
- 1 skein ecru

Lay out the fabric and transfer the design as described on page 10. Vary the angle of each daisy for more interest. Place the fabric in your embroidery hoop.

Use 3 strands of green to embroider the stem, using stem stitch. When you reach a leaf, divert and sew these using lazy daisy stitch.

Change to 3 strands of blue and work the petals in lazy daisy stitch. If you want the petals or leaves to have more weight, sew an additional stitch down the middle of the lazy daisy stitch.

Use 3 strands of yellow to sew French knots, filling the centre of the flower.

For the white daisies, repeat the stems and leaves as before, but work their petals in a raised satin stitch using 3 strands of ecru. This makes them stand out better on the cream background. Embroider the centres in satin stitch, using 3 strands of yellow.

Wash the square to remove any traces of carbon or pen, allow to dry and press.

Make the table cloth. For the border, cut 4 strips of the contrasting fabric 20 cm (8 in) longer than the length of the central square and 20 cm (8 in) deep. This allows enough space to mitre the corners.

Fold the border strips in half lengthways and press with the right sides facing. To mitre the corners, use a protractor or set-square and draw a 45-degree angle from the folded edge to the raw edge with a water-soluble pen. Lay out two strips and with right sides facing, pin and sew together along the drawn lines. Cut away the excess fabric at the corner.

Repeat for the other three corners. Turn right side out. Press along the seams and border. Sew one edge of the border panel to the raw edge of the embroidered square. Fold in the seam allowance on the other side of the border and attach this edge to the square by oversewing by hand. This ensures a neat finish on both sides of the table cloth.

Leafy throw

Leaves can be used very effectively in embroidery. For this throw I used two different leaf designs scattered over a textured fabric. I used the colours of autumn as my inspiration, with rich shades of terracotta for contrast against the cream of the throw. The maple leaves are worked very simply in an outline stitch, which highlights the shape beautifully. The other design is filled in, using satin stitch in complementary shades for added weight. The edges of the throw are finished off with blanket stitch.

Use a ready-made throw or blanket in a textured fabric, but make sure it is a tight weave. Or make one up yourself. I had this textured fabric for ages before I could decide what to do with it. Once I worked out the leaf design, I could see that this fabric would be perfect to set off the leaves.

You will need
1 throw in a close-weave textured fabric
Or 1,5 m (1⅔ yds) square of suitable fabric plus
1,5 m (1⅔ yds) square of contrasting backing fabric
  depending on the size of throw you want.
Leaf templates
Water-soluble pen or dressmaker's carbon paper
Crewel needle size 6
Embroidery hoop
Small sharp scissors
Sewing cotton
Sewing machine

DMC embroidery thread in these colours
4 skeins 3777 dark terracotta
4 skeins 3776 mahogany

Lay out the fabric and use a water-soluble pen to mark where the motifs are to be placed. To make this easier, photocopy each leaf design several times and roughly cut them out. Place each leaf more or less where you feel it should go and mark the spot with a water-soluble pen. Transfer the designs as described on page 10.

Tilt each leaf in a different direction. You can also vary the sizes of the leaves for added interest.

Start with the **maple leaf**, working the stem in couched satin stitch, using 3 strands of DMC 3777. As you move along the stem, sew a single stitch for each vein. Use

3 strands of the same colour to sew around the outline of the leaf, using couched satin stitch.

Using 3 strands of DMC 3777, **sew the stems** of the solid leaf in stem stitch. Embroider each leaflet in satin stitch. Sew one half using 3 strands of DMC 3777 and the other half using DMC 3776. When embroidering the leaves it helps to sew a few running stitches around the outline of the leaf. When you begin the satin stitch, incorporate these stitches underneath. This serves as a useful guide when sewing and also creates a slightly rounded effect on the edge of the leaf.

If you wish to add a border to a ready-made throw, choose one of the leaf colours and sew along the edges using all 6 strands and working in blanket stitch. I only sewed a border along the two short sides. Wash to remove any traces of pen or carbon, allow to dry and press carefully.

Make the throw. Place the 2 squares together, right sides facing and machine-stitch seams all round, leaving an opening in one side. Finish the seams, trim the corners and turn right side out. Press seams and hand-sew opening closed. Machine-stich all round about 10 mm from the edge. To finish off, sew a border along the two short edges in blanket stitch.

Then … snuggle up with a good book, or someone who's read a good book!

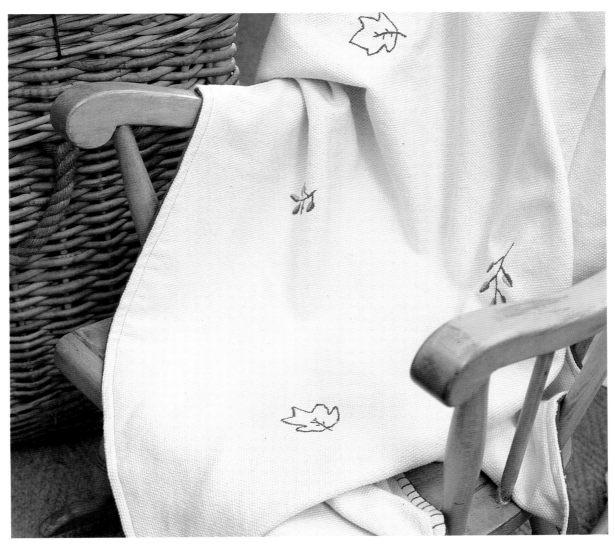

Sprigged cushion

I love cushions, as my family will testify! With cushions you can update the feel of a room, quickly and inexpensively, adapting and changing the colours from season to season. For the embroiderer, cushions provide an ideal base on which to create, and they make great presents too!

Cushions can be made up in all sizes, but for a lounge I like to keep mine large – no smaller than 50 cm (20 in) square, ideal for sinking into on a comfortable sofa.

This cushion has pretty sprigs scattered all over, which are simple to embroider and would make an ideal project for a beginner. You can make up the cushion yourself or buy plain ready-made cushion covers. Wash and iron calico before use.

You will need

55 cm (21½ in) square cream calico
   for cushion front
2 rectangles of cream calico for cushion back,
   one 40 x 55 cm (15½ x 21½ in) and
   the other 25 x 55 cm (10 x 21½ in)
Sewing cotton
Sewing machine
Template of sprigs
Water-soluble pen
Crewel needle size 6
Embroidery hoop
Sharp scissors

DMC embroidery thread in these colours

2 skeins 3777 dark terracotta
1 skein 742 light tangerine
1 skein 602 cranberry
1 skein 3364 pine green

Lay out calico square and mark the postion of the sprigs. Don't place any motifs closer than 3 cm (1¼ in) from the edge to allow for the seam. Transfer the design as described on page 10.

Place the fabric in the embroidery hoop. Using 3 strands of thread, start with DMC 3364 pine green and embroider the stems in stem stitch. Embroider the leaves in satin stitch.

Change to DMC 3777 dark terracotta to work the petals in satin stitch. Make a French knot in either 602 cranberry or 742 light tangerine in the centre. Wash to remove any traces of carbon and pen, allow to dry and iron on the reverse side.

Make the cushion. Hem one 55 cm (21½ in) edge of each backing rectangle. With right sides facing, lay the two rectangles on the cushion front making sure they overlap. If you wish to use piping, tack into position now so it will be incorporated into the seam. Machine stitch, finish seam edges, trim and turn right side out. Press seams. Insert a nice big puffy inner, place on your sofa and watch everyone admire your handiwork!

Topiary tree cushion

These topiary tree designs were inspired by small conifer trees placed on either side of a neighbour's front door. The treetop is worked in couching stitch, which gives it an interesting texture. As my friend Natalie pointed out, they have a Christmas tree look about them and could be used on table linen for a seasonal feel. Although I have used triangles for the treetops, you can really use any shape. Look around for inspiration!

YOU WILL NEED

1 ready-made cushion cover. To make up your own as specified for Sprigged cushion (see page 61)
Template of topiary tree
Water-soluble pen
Tape-measure and ruler
Crewel needle size 6
Embroidery hoop
Sharp embroidery scissors

DMC embroidery thread in the following colours

1 skein 904 dark parrot green
1 skein 838 dark beige brown
1 skein ecru
1 skein 3777 terracotta

Lay out your fabric, find the centre and draw a line 5 cm (2 in) below this with a water-soluble pen. Transfer the design as described on page 10, using this as your baseline. Place one tree in the centre, the other two on either side equally spaced. Place the fabric in the embroidery hoop.

Use 3 strands of DMC 904 green and sew the tree in couching stitch, starting at the top and working from left to right in rows. Keep the lines close together and the stitches even.

To work the stem, soil and shading, change to 3 strands of brown and work in satin stitch. Change to 3 strands of ecru and work the white patch in satin stitch. Work the pot in 3 strands of DMC 3777. First sew the rim of the pot in horizontal long and short stitches, followed by the body in vertical long and short stitches, working the threads into the shading stitches.

Wash to remove all pen marks, allow to dry and press on the reverse side. To make up the cushion, follow the instructions on page 61.

When I worked the couching stitch on the tree, I found it easier to bring the thread out at the left-hand side, insert it on the right and then work back along this line with my single stitches. I repeated this process for the whole treetop.

Daisies on denim

Denim makes a hard-wearing floor-cushion and seemed a sensible choice, as most of my cushions end up on the floor anyway where my children use them as a jungle gym. I decorated the cushion with three funky long-stemmed daisies with crewel-work petals for extra fun. Wash the denim several times before use to prevent dye from spoiling your embroidery. These daisies will look equally effective on bed-linen, towels, bags, anywhere really!

YOU WILL NEED

Blue denim 60 x 75 cm (24 x 29 in),
    plus 2 rectangles, of 60 x 50 cm (25 x 20 in)
    and 60 x 35 cm (25 x 14 in) for backing
Template of daisies
White pencil
Tape-measure and ruler
Crewel needle size 6
Embroidery hoop
Sharp embroidery scissors
Sewing thread
Sewing machine

DMC embroidery thread in the following colours

1 skein 304 medium red
1 skein ecru

Lay your fabric out and transfer the design as described on page 10, using a white pencil. Place the short-stemmed daisy in the middle with two long-stemmed daisies on either side, equally spaced. Place the denim into the embroidery hoop.

Use 3 strands of ecru and work each stem in stem stitch. Also with 3 strands of thread, work each leaf in chain stitch. The veins are worked in fern stitch.

Use 3 strands of ecru thread for the petals. Work the outline of the petal in chain stitch and fill in with 2 lines of chain stitch, using the same thread. Change to 3 strands of dark red and stitch the centre of the daisy in satin stitch.

Make up the cushion cover as described on page 61 and pop in a big soft inner.

Contemporary circle on square cushion

This simple contemporary design was worked on a deep-red bull-denim fabric in a mixture of stranded cotton and metallic thread which adds interest. I find using metallic thread on its own fairly tricky, as the filaments tend to separate. But mixing it with the stranded cotton makes it much easier to work with, while giving a lovely metallic glint to the work.

YOU WILL NEED

55 cm (21½ in) square deep-red bull-denim
2 rectangles of fabric for cushion back,
   one 40 x 55 cm (15½ x 21½ in) and
   the other 25 x 55 cm (10 x 21½ in)
Template of circles
Water-soluble pen
Tape-measure and ruler
Compass
Crewel needle size 6
Embroidery hoop
Sharp embroidery scissors
Sewing thread
Sewing machine
Scissors

DMC embroidery thread in the following colours

1 skein ecru thread
1 skein 5283 silver metallic thread

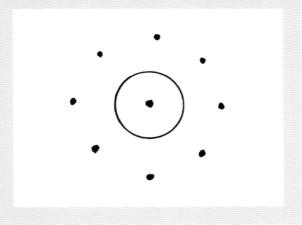

Lay out the fabric and transfer the design as described on page 10. Find the centre-point of the fabric for the French knot in the centre, and use a compass to draw a neat circle.

Using 3 strands of ecru and 1 strand of silver, sew a French knot at the centre. Next work the circle in chain stitch. Finish off by working 8 French knots, spaced equally around the outside of the chain-stitch circle. For a different look you can work the circle in couching stitch.

Wash to remove any pen marks or carbon residue, allow to dry and iron on the reverse side. Follow the instructions on page 61 to make up the cushion.

Sea holly cushion

This beautifully simple design was inspired by the sea holly growing in my garden. Seeding stitch is particularly effective for the light and feathery look of the flowerheads. This design is also striking reduced in size and repeated randomly over the entire cushion cover.

If you are making up your own cushion cover, use a soft viscose or muslin rather than calico to enhance the soft, feminine design.

YOU WILL NEED

1 ready-made cushion cover. To make up your own as specified for Sprigged cushion (see page 61)
Template of sea holly
Water-soluble pen
Crewel needle size 6
Embroidery hoop
Sharp embroidery scissors

DMC embroidery thread in the following colours

1 skein 3816 celadon green
1 skein 209 dark lavender
1 skein 3817 light celadon green

Transfer the design to the cushion-cover front or fabric as described on page 10. Place the fabric in the embroidery hoop.

Using 3 strands of DMC 3816, work the stems in stem stitch. Work the top half of each leaf in fishbone stitch. Change to 3 strands of DMC 3817 and work the bottom half of each leaf in fishbone stitch, working the stitches into the top half of the leaf.

Use 3 strands of DMC 209 lavender and work each head in seeding stitch.

Wash to remove any trace of pen or carbon, allow to dry, press and make up the cushion cover as described on page 61.

Monogrammed cushion with leaf design

A monogram is a lovely way to personalize a piece of linen. For this cushion cover I chose soft viscose with a subtle shine and stitched a delicate leaf design in the centre. The classic shape of the letters used for the initials complement the design beautifully. As with all the cushions, you can either buy a ready-made cover or make up your own.

YOU WILL NEED

Cushion cover or to make up your own, as specified for Sprigged cushion (see page 61)
Leaf template
Letter template (see page 41)
Water-soluble pen
Crewel needle size 6
Embroidery hoop
Scissors
1 skein DMC ecru

Lay out your fabric or cushion cover and mark the centre with a water-soluble pen. Transfer the leaf design as described on page 10 with the initials in position underneath. Place the fabric or cushion cover in the embroidery hoop.

Use 3 strands of ecru and stitch each leaf in raised satin stitch. Keep the stitches small and close together, ensuring that no fabric shows through underneath. Work the stem in stem stitch.

Embroider each initial in couched satin stitch. For the wider part of the letters, work the satin stitch over 2 lines of vertical running stitches (see page 40).

When working the leaves, first stitch around the outline in small running stitches and then use satin stitch to fill in the leaves, stitching over the line of running stitches. This gives a slightly raised effect that shows off the silky look of the embroidery thread.

Hot chilli on adjustable apron

Vegetables are fun to embroider. This chilli is very simple, but really brightens up the cream calico of the adjustable apron. Embroidering *hot!* underneath adds a bit of humour. It will also work well on tea-towels, serviettes and tablecloths. I've even been tempted to use it on a T-shirt for a friend, adding *stuff* to *hot!*

I like to wear an apron when I cook – it puts me in the mood for cooking. This apron is longer than normal, as that's the way I like them, but I made it with an adjustable draw-string, so the length can be adjusted up or down. The lime-green casing for the drawstring adds some extra colour.

These aprons are one of my best sellers and have made great gifts for friends.

You will need

1,3 x 1 m (51 x 39 in) calico or bull-denim
15 x 40 cm (6 x 15½ in) gingham for casing,
  cut on the bias
4 m (4¼ yds) woven tape 3 cm (1¼ in) wide
Template of apron pattern
Template of chilli
Water-soluble pen
Tape-measure
Crewel needle size 6
Embroidery hoop
Sharp embroidery scissors
Sewing thread
Sewing machine

DMC embroidery thread in the following colours

1 skein 321 red
1 skein 902 dark garnet
1 skein ecru
1 skein 907 light parrot green

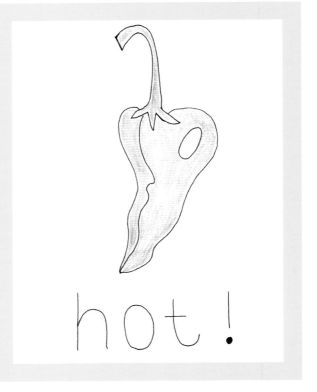

Make the apron. Use the template to draw the pattern full size onto paper and cut out. Fold your fabric in half and lay the pattern on the fold. Adjust the length if necessary and cut out.

Machine stitch a 1 cm (½ in) hem along all the straight edges. Fold the gingham in half lengthways and cut. Fit to the curved edges and machine stitch a small hem along the short sides, adjusting the length if required. With right sides facing, sew each gingham strip to a curved edge. Fold over to the back of the apron and press. Press a neat hem in the raw edge of the gingham. Machine stitch gingham casing down, taking in hem, making sure that the edges where the tape will pass through are neat.

Use a safety pin to thread the tape through the casing, forming a loop for the neck edge. Trim if necessary and knot the ends.

Embroider the chilli. Lay out the apron and transfer the design as described on page 10. Place the apron in your Embroidery hoop.

Stitch the stem in couched satin stitch, using 3 strands of green. Work the bottom of the stem in satin stitch only. Change to 3 strands of ecru and work the highlight in long and short stitch. Use 3 strands of dark red and work the dark shading in long and short stitch. Finally, with 3 strands of lighter red, stitch the remaining area of the chilli in long and short stitch.

Now stitch the word *hot!* using 3 strands of dark red and working in couched satin stitch. Keep each stitch small, tight and evenly spaced.

Rinse off any pen marks and cook up a curry!

You can make a similar apron for a child. Adjust the apron template and choose a suitable design. My daughter has an apron with a cerise-pink sheep on it.

When sewing long and short stitch, don't have your material too tight in your hoop. Otherwise it could pucker.

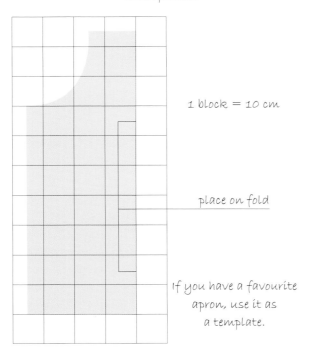

1 block = 10 cm

place on fold

If you have a favourite apron, use it as a template.

Pig, cow & sheep on denim apron

My friend Natalie has a thing about cows. They are everywhere and add a humorous touch to her kitchen. So this apron was made with her in mind. I just had to add a sheep and pig for a bit of variety. The apron itself is made up in blue denim, a nice hard-wearing fabric. This one is not adjustable, so it's even easier to make up yourself.

You will need

1,3 x 1,0 m (51 x 39½ in) blue denim
2½ m (2¾ yds) woven tape 3 cm (1¼ in) wide
Template of apron pattern (see page 69)
Templates of pig, cow and sheep
Tape-measure
Dressmaker's carbon paper and white pencil
Crewel needle size 6
Embroidery hoop
Sharp embroidery scissors
Sewing cotton
Sewing machine

DMC embroidery thread in the following colours

2 skeins ecru
1 skein 310 black
1 skein 3805 cyclamen pink
1 skein 353 peach
1 skein 414 steel gray

Make the apron as described on page 68 for chilli apron, but omit casing for adjustable neck and ties and include a 1 cm (½ in) hem for the curved edges, taking care not to stretch the fabric. Cut a length of tape for the neck edge and machine stitch to the top of the apron (see photograph). Halve the rest of the tape and machine stitch to the top edge of either side for the waist. Knot the ends.

Wash the apron several times to ensure that the dye will not run into your embroidered designs and spoil them.

Transfer the design. Lay out the apron and mark with your pencil where the motifs are to be placed. Use dressmaker's carbon-paper to copy the design and trace over with white pencil which will show up more clearly on the denim.

Embroider the pig. Frame the pig in your embroidery hoop and work each eye and the nostrils as French knots, using 3 strands of black.

Change to 3 strands of DMC 3805 cyclamen pink and stitch the nose in satin stitch, taking care to stitch around the nostrils. Using the same colour, stitch each ear in satin stitch. Sew the four legs as a single straight stitch and the tail in couched satin stitch, following the curve as you sew. Change to 3 strands of DMC 414 grey and work each spot in satin stitch.

Embroider the body and face in 3 strands of DMC 353 peach using long and short stitch, sewing around the eyes, nostrils and grey spots.

Embroider the sheep. Use 3 strands of black and work each eye as a French knot. Sew each ear as a lazy daisy stitch. Using 3 strands of DMC 353 peach, work the nose in satin stitch, and each leg as a single straight stitch. The body is worked using all 6 strands of ecru

thread in tightly spaced French knots. Take care not to sew over the eyes.

Embroider the cow. Work each eye as a French knot, using 3 strands of black. Now sew the black spots in satin stitch. Change to DMC 353 peach and work the nose and the udders in satin stitch with a single stitch for the teats. Work the face and body in long and short stitch, using 3 strands of ecru thread. Each ear is two straight stitches worked in 3 strands of ecru.

The tail and legs are also worked with 3 strands of ecru thread in straight stitch. The tail has 5 tiny stitches at the end to simulate hair.

Orange-tree tea-cosy

This orange-tree design has been used to great effect to decorate a tea-cosy. The leaves have been worked in lightweight, dark green perlé cotton, which gives them a glossy sheen. The rest of the tree is worked in stranded embroidery cotton. Although I embroidered oranges, you could make it a lemon-tree, an apple-tree or any other fruit-tree.

You will need

Fabric for the outer cosy
Lining (twice as much as for outer) and wadding
Paper for cosy template
Template of orange tree
Water-soluble pen
Tape-measure
Crewel needle size 6
Embroidery hoop
Sharp embroidery scissors
Sewing cotton
Sewing machine

DMC embroidery thread in the following colours

1 skein 721 orange spice
1 skein ecru
1 skein 3777 terra cotta
1 skein Coton Perlé no 5, mid-green
1 skein 3371 black brown
1 skein 904 dark parrot green

Use your teapot as a guide for size and make a paper template for the cosy. Cut out and pin to fabric for outer cosy. Cut two. Transfer the design onto one of the cosy outers as described on page 10. Place the fabric in the embroidery hoop.

Embroider the orange tree. Using 3 strands of ecru stitch the highlight on each orange and on the pot in satin stitch. Change to 3 strands of orange and embroider each orange in satin stitch, working around the ecru shading.

Now use the green Coton Perlé to work each leaf in satin stitch. Change to 3 strands of DMC green and work the stem in small even satin stitches.

With 3 strands of dark brown, work the shading of the pot and the soil in horizontal long and short stitch. Stitch up the side of the stem in a line of stem stitches.

Change to DMC 3777 terracotta and stitch the rest of the pot in horizontal long and short stitch.

Make the tea cosy. Pin template to lining fabric and cut 4, adding a 1 cm (½ in) seam allowance. Trim template by 1 cm along the straight edge, place on the wadding and and cut 2. Machine stitch two pairs of lining together, right sides facing, leaving the straight edge open. Turn right side out and insert the wadding. Fold in raw edges and machine stitch the bottom edge.

Place cosy outers together, right sides facing, and machine stitch, leaving the straight edge open. Trim seam, cutting notches along curve. Machine stitch wadded linings together, leaving the straight edge open. Trim seam, cutting notches along curve. Place cosy outer in lining. Stitch together straight edge, leaving an opening to turn right side out. Turn right side out and hand-sew opening close. Press seams.

Wash to remove any pen or carbon marks.

Make yourself a pot of tea, open the chocolate biscuits, and admire your handiwork!

Bugs on a tea-towel

Drying dishes is a fact of life in most homes and although dish cloths are utility items, they can be made attractive and fun with embroidery.

This tongue-in-cheek design uses all the bugs we don't normally want in our kitchens, such as ants, wasps, flies and beetles, which are worked between the vertical borders of a ready-made tea-towel.

The tea-towel I used has two decorative blue lines on it. I placed my designs vertically between these lines, alternating the bugs on the opposite side.

You will need

1 tea-towel
Template of bugs
Water-soluble pen
Tape-measure
Crewel needle size 6
Embroidery hoop
Sharp embroidery scissors

DMC embroidery thread in the following colours

1 skein 3750 dark antique blue
1 skein 906 parrot green
1 skein 340 blue violet
1 skein 524 light fern green
1 skein 725 topaz (yellow)
Black sewing cotton

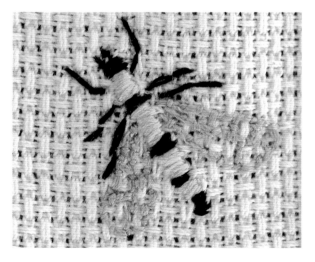

Lay out the tea-towel and mark where the designs are to be placed using a tape-measure and water-soluble pen. Transfer the design as described on page 10. Place the tea towel in your embroidery hoop.

Embroider the ant. Using 3 strands of dark blue, work two straight stitches for the antennae. Stitch the head and thorax in satin stitch. Work the abdomen in long and short stitch. Work each leg in couching stitch. Keep the stitches close together to create a solid line.

Embroider the fly. Using 2 strands of ordinary black cotton, stitch the antennae in straight stitch. Now work each leg in couching stitch. Change to fern green and use 3 strands to work each wing, using couching stitch for the outline and straight stitch for the veins.

Finally, change to 3 strands of parrot green and work the body in satin stitch, stitching in any loose threads from the legs and wings. This ensures a neat effect on the reverse side of the tea-towel.

Embroider the wasp. Using 2 strands of black sewing cotton, stitch the antennae in straight stitch. Work the head and black stripes on the body in satin stitch and the legs in couching stitch. Change to fern green and work the wings in couching stitch and the veins in straight stitches. Finally, change to yellow and work the yellow stripes as satin stitch, sewing in any loose threads as you go.

Embroider the beetle. Using 2 strands of ordinary black cotton, stitch the antennae in straight stitch, the head in satin stitch, and the legs in couching stitch. Change to DMC 340 blue violet and work the abdomen in long and short stitch, sewing in any loose threads from the legs and head.

Wash the tea towel to remove pen or carbon marks, allow to dry and offer it to your partner the next time he dries the dishes.

Veggies on a tea-towel

These stylised vegetables are bright and easy to embroider onto a ready-made plain white tea-towel. They will also look great embroidered individually onto serviettes or an apron, and in a central and border pattern on a tablecloth. The tea-towel I used has two decorative green lines on it. I placed the motifs vertically between these lines.

YOU WILL NEED

1 tea-towel
Template of vegetables
Water-soluble pen
Tape-measure
Crewel needle size 6
Embroidery hoop
Sharp embroidery scissors

DMC embroidery thread for the red chilli, red pepper and tomato in these colours

1 skein 666 bright red
1 skein 3777 terracotta
1 skein 902 dark garnet
1 skein 906 parrot green

For the yellow chilli

1 skein 904 dark parrot green
1 skein 725 topaz (yellow)

For the aubergine or brinjal

1 skein 902 dark garnet
1 skein 906 parrot green

For the olive

1 skein 470 light avocado green
1 skein 934 black avocado green

For the carrot

1 skein 906 parrot green
1 skein 900 dark orange
1 skein 970 light pumpkin

For the green chilli

1 skein 934 black avocado green
1 skein 904 dark parrot green
1 skein ecru for all the high-lights

Lay out the tea-towel, carefully measure and mark where each vegetable should go and transfer the design as described on page 10. Place the tea towel in your embroidery hoop.

Embroider the tomato. Using 3 strands of DMC 906 green, work the stem in stem stitch. Fill in the leaves on the top of the tomato using satin stitch.

Work the highlight in 3 strands of ecru, using satin stitch. Change to 3 strands of DMC 3777 terracotta and work dark shading in long and short stitch. Use 3 strands of DMC 666 red to stitch the rest of the tomato in long and short stitch.

Embroider the yellow chilli. Use 3 strands of DMC 904 dark green and work the stem and dark shading in long and short stitch. Work the highlight in 3 strands of ecru, using satin stitch. Use 3 strands of DMC 725 yellow to work the main body of the chilli in long and short stitch.

Embroider the red pepper. Using 3 strands of DMC 906 green, work the stem in long and short stitch. Work the highlight in 3 strands of ecru, using satin stitch. Change to 3 strands of DMC 902 and work a line of long and short stitches in the dark shade areas. Use DMC 3777 for the lighter areas also in long and short stitch. Finally, use 3 strands of DMC 666 and work the rest of the pepper in long and short stitch.

Embroider the brinjal. Stitch the stem in long and short stitch, using 3 strands of DMC 906 green. Work the highlight in 3 strands of ecru, using satin stitch. Now use 3 strands of DMC 902 and work the remaining area of the aubergine in long and short stitch.

Embroider the olives. Using 3 strands of DMC 470 light green, work each stem in couched satin stitch and each leaf in fishbone stitch. Stitch the light green area on the front olive in satin stitch (see template). Work the high-light in 3 strands of ecru, using satin stitch. Now change to 3 strands of DMC 934 and work the rest of each olive in long and short stitch.

Embroider the carrot in rows of couching stitch to give it an interesting texture. Use 3 strands of DMC 906 green

and work the top in couched satin stitch. The featherlike leaves are worked in single stitches. Work the highlight on the carrot in 3 strands of ecru, using satin stitch. Now using DMC 970 light orange, work the body of the carrot in couching stitch. Keep the rows close together. Change to DMC 900 dark orange and work a line of stem stitch along the left-hand edge of the carrot.

Embroider the red chilli. Work the stem in long and short stitch using 3 strands of DMC 906 green. Work the highlight in 3 strands of ecru, using satin stitch. Using 3 strands of DMC 3777 terracotta, sew the area of dark shading in long and short stitch. Now sew the remaining part of the chilli in DMC 666 red.

Embroider the green chilli. Using DMC 934 dark green, work the stem in couched satin stitch, and the leaf in fishbone stitch. Work the highlight in 3 strands of ecru, using satin stitch. Work the rest of the chilli in long and short stitch, using 3 strands of DMC 904 dark parrot green.

These veggies taste great when dribbled with olive oil and a splash of balsamic vinegar and roasted in the oven. Serve with couscous or pasta. Delicious!

Bees on a fly-net

We love to eat al fresco on nice summer days, but have a bit of a problem with flies. I made this fly-net using ordinary netting, and to jazz it up a bit, added bees embroidered in French knots. The French knots work well on the netting and make the bees look very tactile and friendly. I used a decorative edging for the border, but if you feel very creative, you could add a border of beads which will give the net extra weight.

You will need

1 m (36 in) square white netting
4 m (4 yds) decorative edging
Water-soluble pen
Bee template
Crewel needle size 6
Embroidery hoop
Scissors

DMC embroidery thread in the following colours

1 skein 310 black
1 skein 725 topaz (yellow)
1 skein 3864 light beige

Lay out the netting and transfer the design as described on page 10. I scattered the bees over the netting randomly and also made them different sizes.

Place the netting in your embroidery hoop, taking great care not to stretch it. Using all 6 strands of thread, work the black sections in French knots. Change to 6 strands of yellow and work the sections as French knots.

To work the wings, change to 3 strands of DMC 3864 beige and work the outline of the wings in couched satin stitch. Work the veins on the wings in the same way. Finally, use 3 strands of black to work the antennae in couched satin stitch.

Sew on the decorative edging by hand or machine and rinse off any pen marks.

Using tapestry wool for the bees' bodies will make them even more tactile. Muslin can be used instead of netting.

Silver twigs on black velvet evening bag

When I asked my mum what she wanted for Christmas, she asked for an evening bag. I took a look around the shops and became inspired to make one for her. I searched in my fabric collection and found some black velvet that would be ideal. This just called for a simple, elegant design using metallic embroidery thread. The bag is lined with an iridescent viscose fabric for a professional finish. The finished bag looked just as good as any shop-bought bag and was made at a fraction of the cost.

You WILL NEED

50 cm (18 in) black velvet or other suitable fabric (115 cm (45 in) wide)
Lining as above
Cord or piping
Sewing machine
Black sewing cotton
White pencil
Template of twigs
Ruler
Crewel needle size 6
Embroidery hoop
Sharp embroidery scissors
1 skein DMC 5283 silver

Cut fabric for bag 44 x 18 cm (17¼ x 7 in). This includes a seam allowance. Fold over with the short sides together. Lightly mark where the design is to be placed, using a white pencil. Copy the design onto the fabric, varying the heights. Place the fabric in the embroidery hoop, taking care not to crush the velvet.

Use 3 strands of DMC 5283 and work the stem from the bottom up in stem stitch. As you reach each stalk, sew a single stitch and finish it off with a French knot. Then return to the stem and continue.

Mixing the metallic thread with strands of ordinary embroidery cotton, for example 2 strands of DMC ecru to 1 strand of metallic, makes it easier to work with. This still gives a metallic sheen. Work the French knots in silver thread only. Alternatively, work the entire project in couched satin stitch, just using French knots on the end of each stalk. You will use more thread this way, but it does make working with the silver thread a little easier.

To make the bag. Cut lining the same size as the velvet. Place lining and velvet together, right sides facing. Machine stitch 3 sides together, leaving one end open. Finish and trim seams and corners. Turn right side out. Fold over so that the embroidered side is facing in and the lining is on the outside. Stitch together the sides, using a zig-zag stitch on your sewing machine. Turn right side out and push out the corners.

Cut a strip of velvet 36 x 5 cm (14 x 2 in). Pin and tack to the top of the bag, right sides facing (as if sewing on a waistband) and stitch. Fold over and hand sew in position, preferably using hemstitch.

Cut two strips of velvet for the handles to the desired length. I made mine 53 cm (21 in) which is long enough for the bag to be worn over the shoulder, as is the current fashion for small handbags

Cut two lengths of cord the same length as the handles. Enclose the cord in the velvet strips, folding in the raw edges, and machine stitch close to the edge. Sew the handles on securely.

For slimmer, more elegant handles, pull the velvet tight around the cord and use a hemming stitch to sew in any excess fabric along the length of each handle.

If you wish to close the opening you could do so with small strips of black Velcro.

DO NOT iron velvet, as it will crush and leave shiny patches.

Snooze-pillows and other sweet-smelling gifts

Lavender is well known for its sleep-inducing and calming properties. So why not use it in a snooze-pillow. The snooze-pillow was embroidered with lavender sprigs (see page 18), then filled with dried lavender heads and cotton scraps sprinkled with lavender essential oil. Other herbs you can use are camomile, rosemary, lemon verbena, cloves and scented geraniums. Also make small sachets, embroidered with a pretty design of your choice, and fill them with a mixture of dried herbs. The embroidered lavender bags make lovely gifts, and have been one of my best sellers at craft markets. You could make several, embroidered with different designs and tied with ribbon.

You will need

2 x 25 cm (9 in) square pieces of white cotton
   or voile
Water-soluble pen
Template of your choice
Embroidery thread as for chosen design
Stitches as for chosen design
Dried lavender or other herbs
Sewing machine
Sewing cotton

Cut lavender after any dew has lifted, but before the sun gets too hot, as the oil content is highest in the early morning. Try to cut the flowers with longish stalks and handle the flowers as little as possible. Tie the stems together and hang to dry in a dark place. (The darker the drying area, the better the lavender heads will retain their colour.) Once the lavender is dry, pick off the flower heads and separate the petals. Place these in a sieve and shake off any dust (try to do this outside, as the dust can be an irritant). This process separates the petals nicely. Use this as a filling for the lavender bags and snooze-pillow. To store, place in an airtight jar with orris-root or sea salt as a fixative.

Choose a design, lay out one square of fabric and transfer the design as described on page 10. Place the fabric in the embroidery hoop and embroider as described for that particular design.

To make the snooze-pillow. Lay the two pieces of fabric together with right sides facing and machine stitch, leaving an opening to turn right side out. Finish and trim seams and corners and turn right side out. Press seams. Fill with your dried herbs, then sew up the opening using hemstitch.

Alternatively, machine stitch a border around the outside edge of the pillow, using zig-zag stitch.

To make herb sachets. Make smaller versions of the snooze-pillow – 12 cm (5 in) square is a good size. Use a pretty fabric on one side of the sachet and embroidery on the other. First do the embroidery and then cut to size.

When I have completed orders of bed-linen, I usually make a lavender sachet with the same design embroidered on and slip it among the folds of the linen. This is usually greeted with more delight than the bed-linen itself! A nice touch if you are giving embroidered linen as a gift (especially if the recipient is an insomniac).

To make lavender bags. Follow the instructions for the snooze-pillow, but stitch togeher only three sides. Make a casing at the opening and insert a thin cord or ribbon. Knot the ends and pull tight to close.

If you are using a combination of herbs, first mix these up in a bowl. Pour the mixture into your sachets or bags, using a paper funnel, and then sew closed.

Embroidered drawstring bags

I find these drawstring bags endlessly useful for storing anything from toilet rolls to socks! I make them up in different sizes – from small ones for dried lavender heads and other herbs that I hang from hangers in my wardrobe, to large laundry-bags. They can be made up in a variety of fabrics from cotton to voile and make great gifts. My friend Jane got a monogrammed bag for Christmas. You can use the template and embroidery instructions for any design in the book or make up your own designs. I've often intended to do a washing-line with various articles of clothing on a laundry-bag to identify the contents of the bag. Or make this fun bag with two giraffes, one looking rather surprised at being bright purple and pink. The tree is appliquéd, using lime green gingham.

You will need

Cotton or voile for the size of bag required
Length of cord twice the width of the bag
Template of giraffes and tree
Scrap of fabric for treetop appliqué
Water-soluble pen
Tape-measure
Crewel needle size 6
Embroidery hoop
Sharp embroidery scissors
Sewing machine
Sewing cotton

DMC embroidery thread in the following colours

1 skein 907 light parrot green
1 skein 3371 black brown
1 skein 3805 cyclamen pink (giraffe spots)
1 skein 340 blue violet (giraffe body)
1 skein 606 bright orange-red (giraffe body)
1 skein 3828 hazelnut brown (giraffe spots)

Lay out the fabric and transfer the design as described on page 10, preferably towards the bottom of the bag so that the motifs will be visible even when the bag is closed. Place the fabric in the embroidery hoop.

Cut out the treetop shape from the scrap of fabric you are using for appliqué. Use 3 strands of DMC 3371 dark brown to work the tree trunk in long and short stitch. Pin the treetop shape to the top of the tree and stitch on, using 3 strands of green and satin stitch.

Change to 3 strands of black and embroider the eye of each giraffe as a French knot.

Work the tails in straight stitch. Stitch an exclamation mark in black over the brightly coloured giraffe. The ears are worked in lazy daisy stitch.

Change to 3 strands of the colour for the spots and sew them in satin stitch. Repeat for the other giraffe.

Use 3 strands to embroider the body in long and short stitch, working around each dot, and repeat for the other giraffe. Finally, use 3 strands of green and straight stitches to work the grass.

To make the basic bag. Cut the fabric to the desired size with a backing and machine stitch 3 sides with right sides facing. Alternatively cut a rectangle, fold in half with right sides facing and machine-stitch 2 sides, leaving an opening at the top. Finish and trim seams and corners. Press a small hem in the open edge then fold over 7 cm (2¾ in) and stitch down. Stitch again 3 cm (1¼ in) from the top.

Turn the bag right side out and carefully unpick the stitching between the two rows of stitches along one seam. Cut the cord to the desired length and thread through the casing with a safety pin. Knot the two ends of the cord and pull to close the bag.

You can also make the casing in a contrasting fabric, such as gingham.

Simple daisies on a duffle bag

This duffle bag can be taken anywhere – to school for sports clothes, to the beach, when you go shopping – and will make a great gift for an older child. It is made up in dark blue bull-denim and lined with cotton, which is optional. Lining it just gives it more body and makes it more hard-wearing. I stitched a very simple star-daisy design on the outside of the bag in cream thread that looks very effective against the dark background.

If you are making the bag as a gift for a new mother, embroider it with teddy bears or another suitable theme so that it can be used as a nappy bag. Adding a plastic lining may be a good idea.

YOU WILL NEED

1 m x 50 cm (39½ x 19¾ in) dark blue bull-denim
1 m x 50 cm (39½ x 19¾ in) lining fabric
   (gingham or stripes will look great)
2 m (78¾ in) cord
2 toggle grips big enough for your cord to go
   through (a plastic grip-and-release device used
   on the cords of rucksaks, available from most
   haberdashery shops)
Sewing cotton
Sewing machine
White pencil

Template of daisies
Ruler
Crewel needle size 6
Embroidery hoop
Sharp embroidery scissors
1 skein DMC ecru

Lay out the fabric for the outside of the bag and cut two rectangles 35 x 50 cm (14 x 20 in), adjusting the size if you wish. Cut two rectangles of lining to the same size.

Draw the design on one side of the bag fabric. Use a white pencil to show up on the denim, and a ruler to ensure an equal distance between motifs.

Place the fabric in your embroidery hoop and use 3 strands of ecru to stitch a French knot in the centre of the design. Using the same length of thread, stitch each petal as a lazy daisy stitch. Secure the ends by oversewing them at the back of the French knot.

Repeat this for all the daisies.

To make the bag. Place denim rectangles together right sides facing. Cut a small length of cord 5 cm long and insert this in a loop at the bottom of one side seam with the ends in line with the raw edge of the fabric. Machine stitch side and bottom seams. Finish and trim seams and corners and turn right side out.

Repeat with the lining, but omit cord and don't turn right side out. Place the lining inside the denim bag and stitch together at the top, leaving an opening to turn right side out. Turn right side out and hand-sew opening closed. To make the casing, fold over 2,5 cm (1 in) and machine stitch.

Unpick the side seam stitching in the casing on the side where the loop was inserted at the bottom. Using a safety pin, thread the cord through the casing. Thread the cord through the single loop at the bottom of the bag, knot the ends and attach a toggle grip to each end. These allow you to adjust the length of the cord quickly and easily.

List of stitches

This is a list of stitches that are used throughout the book. If you are trying a stitch for the first time it is a good idea to first practise on a scrap of fabric.

BACK STITCH

This stitch is sometimes used in embroidery to make a solid, fine line. The stitches are kept small and even.

To sew

Bring the needle out to the front of the fabric and make a small stitch backwards, bringing the needle out on the wrong side. Now make a long stitch forwards bringing your needle out again at the front of the work. Insert the needle slightly to the left of your first stitch, effectively joining the two stitches together, and repeat.

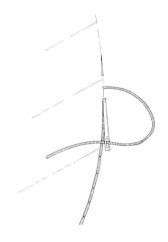

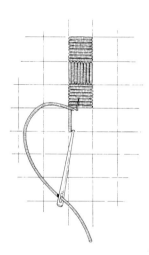

BASKET STITCH

This is a simple stitch used to create a basket-pattern effect. It was commonly used in Jacobean embroidery.

To sew

I find this is best worked between two lines about 1 cm (½ in.) apart. Use your water-soluble pen to draw these lines across the area to be filled.

Use alternating groups of horizontal and vertical satin stitches to create a basket-like effect.

BLANKET STITCH

This stitch is commonly used along the edges of blankets to secure raw edges. It also adds a decorative touch, especially when worked in a contrasting colour to your fabric.

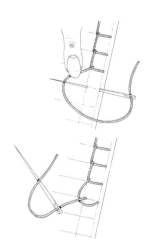

To sew

Draw 2 parallel lines with your water-soluble pen. This helps to keep the stitches the same length. Bring the thread through on the bottom line and hold it down with your left thumb. Insert it again a little to the right on the top line. Bring the needle out again on the bottom line, passing the needle over the held thread. This makes a loop. Pull the thread through until the loop lies flat and tight. Repeat, working to the right.

Chain stitch

This is an attractive stitch that can be used for outlines as I have done for some of the projects, or even as an interesting filling stitch. It consists of a series of loops linked together with a single stitch.

To sew

Bring the thread out at the top of the line to be sewn. Hold the thread down towards you with your left thumb. Insert the needle again to the right-hand side of the point where your thread first emerged. Bring it out again a short distance below, to the length of the stitch you require, passing the needle over the thread you are holding with your thumb. Pull the thread through until you have a flat loop. Hold the thread down again and insert your needle to the right of where the thread emerged inside the loop.

Repeat the stitch, ensuring that all your stitches are the same length.

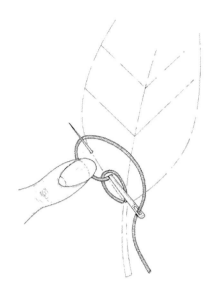

Chevron stitch

This stitch has been used to create attractive borders on various projects in this book.

To sew

First draw two parallel lines onto your fabric using a water-soluble pen.

Starting on the lower line make a back stitch to the right. Bring the needle out in the middle of this stitch.

The next stitch is made by taking the thread to the top line over to the right.

The needle enters the fabric at the spot that will be the centre of the horizontal stitch and emerges to the left (see illustration). Make a stitch along this line, an equal distance to the right. Bring the needle out in the middle of this stitch.

Take the needle down to the bottom line and form the bottom horizontal stitch in the same way to create a zig-zag effect.

COUCHING

This is a technique whereby a thick trailing thread is stitched down at equal intervals with another, fine thread. You can use contrasting colours for an interesting effect. It is also useful when working curved lines.

To sew

Bring out the threads to be held down at the beginning of the line and lay them along the fabric. Unthread the needle.

Thread another needle with your embroidery thread and sew small, evenly spaced, vertical stitches along the length of the loose thread, holding the loose thread with your thumb. It may help to indicate the position of each vertical stitch with your water-soluble pen to ensure that all the stitches are equally spaced.

Before you reach the end of the line, sew the loose threads through to the wrong side of the fabric and work them into the back stitching to secure.

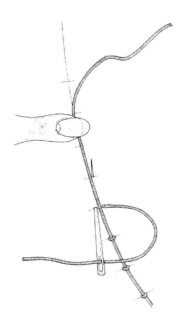

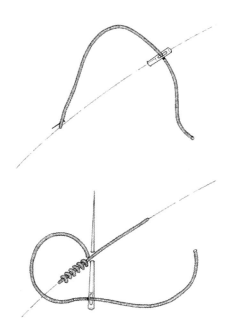

COUCHED SATIN STITCH

Also known as trailing stitch, this differs from couching in that the vertical holding stitches are placed much closer together than in satin stitch, hence the name Couched satin stitch. It's a wonderful stitch to use when you want to create a neat solid-looking curved line.

To sew

For a short line, bring your foundation thread out at the beginning of the line or curve to be stitched. Insert it again at the end. Bring the needle back out to the front of the work at the exact spot the thread first emerged. Now stitch over the foundation threads using tiny satin stitches. If the line has to follow a curve, guide the foundation thread with your thumb.

If you are working a long curved line, bring the foundation threads out at the beginning of the line, and then unthread them. Lay them flat along the top of the fabric. Thread your needle with the thread you are using to sew over the foundation thread and cover with satin stitch. Use your thumb to guide the foundation thread as you sew.

Fern stitch

This is a beautifully simple stitch used to create leaf-veins or fern-like sprays. It is made up of 3 stitches radiating from a single point.

To sew

Using your water-soluble pen, mark a stitch down the central line. Bring the needle out at the bottom of this mark.

Insert it again at a 45-degree angle to the right-hand side. Bring the needle out again at the top of your first stitch. Insert the needle down the central line at the bottom of the first stitch.

Bring it out again at a 45-degree angle to the left of the central line and then insert the needle on the central line where the stitches meet. Pull the thread through. Bring your needle out on the central line at the bottom position of the second stitch. Repeat this process along the line, working from right to left, keeping the stitches an equal length.

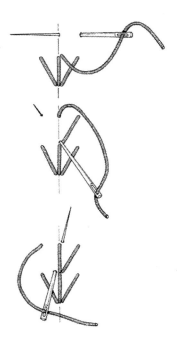

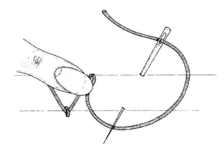

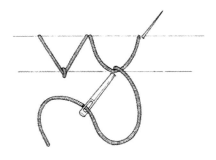

Fly stitch

This stitch can be used on its own as a border stitch, or in rows as a filling stitch. It is generally worked across two lines, which are used as guides.

To sew

Using your water-soluble pen and ruler, draw two straight lines across the fabric, as wide apart as you require the border to be.

Bring the needle out on the top line. Hold the thread with your thumb and insert the needle along this line to the right, turning the needle towards you.

Imagine a V shape. Bring the needle out at the base of the V. Make a small vertical tying stitch over this V, inserting the needle on the bottom line. Repeat.

You can vary the length of the tying stitch to produce different effects.

Fishbone stitch

This stitch creates an attractive herringbone effect, which looks great when sewing leaves.

To sew

Make a small straight stitch from the tip of the leaf a little way down the central vein.

Bring the needle out on the right-hand side and insert it again to the bottom of this first stitch to the left-hand side (see illustration).

Bring the needle out on the left-hand side and insert it at the bottom of the first stitch, this time to the right side of it, crossing over the last two stitches. Continue down the leaf, crossing over the stitches to create a plaited effect, which nicely emphasises the central vein.

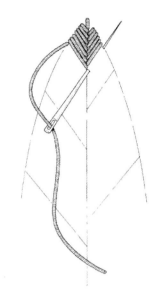

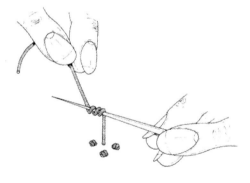

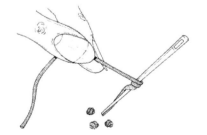

French knots

This very useful stitch is great for creating extra texture, such as on the woolly sheep and in the centres of flowers. Used singly, it can look like a small bead or eye.

To sew

Bring the needle through to the front of the work at the place where the knot or knots are to be placed. Use your left hand to hold the thread taut and wind the thread around your needle, once for a small knot or more for a bigger knot. I normally wind mine round twice for a biger knot.

Turn the needle round and insert it next to where the thread first came out, still holding the thread taut. Pull the needle through releasing the thread at the last minute.

Lazy daisy stitch

This is one of my favourites and great for making petals. It looks like a single chain stitch, and is sometimes known as detached chain stitch.

To sew

Bring the thread out at the bottom of where the stitch is to be placed. Hold the thread down with your left thumb. Insert the needle in the spot where the thread first emerged and pull the needle through while still holding the thread with your left thumb, making a small loop. Bring the needle out at the top of and inside the loop and insert it again, making a small vertical stitch over the thread.

For added effect this single stitch could be worked in a different colour.

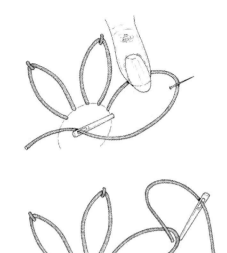

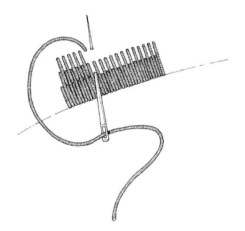

Long and short stitch

This stitch is used to fill in large areas with embroidery thread. It can be worked horizontally or vertically.

To sew

Sew a row of satin stitches along the outline of the work making one long and one short. Keep the outline even. Then work a row of evenly sized satin stitches, fitting them into the spaces left by the short stitches.

Continue in this way until your space is filled.

Raised satin stitch

When you wish to give extra definition to motifs such as leaves or petals, this is the stitch to use.

To sew

Make a line of running stitches around the outline of your shape and then fill in the centre with more running stitches. Stitch over these stitches with satin stitch.

Running stitch

A very simple stitch which consists of a line of stitches of even size and length.

To sew

Run the needle through the fabric, making the stitches an even length to create a broken line of stitches.

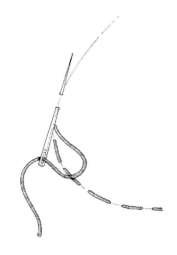

Satin stitch

Satin stitch is a very common embroidery stitch that looks easier than it really is. It is generally used when filling in small areas. It doesn't really work over large areas, as the bigger stitches can look loose and untidy. The trick is to keep the stitches even, parallel and close together so that no fabric shows through.

Having said that, satin stitch can be used over large areas, but then the space should be divided up and the direction of stitches changed, which can produce an interesting effect.

To sew

Start with the needle coming out to the front of the work at the bottom line of the area to be sewn. Insert it again at the top line making a small stitch across the area. Bring the needle out again at the bottom line next to the stitch you have just made. Repeat until the area is filled. The angle of the first stitch will determine how the rest of the stitches will lie. Do not overlap the stitches and keep them smooth and neat.

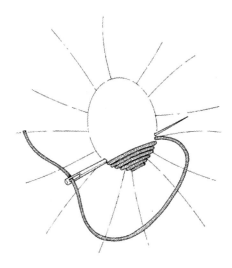

Seeding stitch

These tiny stitches worked at different angles produce a very interesting effect. They can be used as filling stitches, or for flower heads as I have done in this book.

To sew

Sew tiny stitches of more or less even length irregularly over the area to be filled.

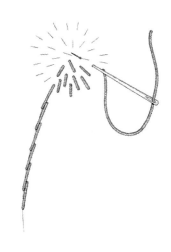

Star stitch

This effective star stitch is simply a series of cross stitches worked over one another. They can be grouped together for an interesting filling stitch or look equally effective when scattered singly over a cushion cover.

To sew

Make a set of cross stitches and place another set of cross stitches diagonally over the first set.

Make two stitches over the intersection of the four crosses, tying them together.

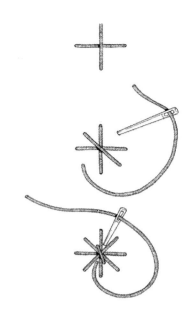

Stem stitch

This stitch is generally used, as its name suggests, when working stems, but it also works very well as an outline stitch. The stitches overlap one another to create an unbroken line.

To sew

Bring the needle out at the front of the fabric to the left of your working line. Insert it again a little way along the line, but this time to the right-hand side, making a small slanted stitch. Pull the needle through, take the needle back and bring it through again about half way along the previous stitch and repeat, keeping the stitches even.

To make a thicker line, vary the angle of the stitches.

Straight stitch

This is simply one single flat stitch.

To sew

Bring the needle through to the front of the fabric. Insert it again, making a single stitch of any length.

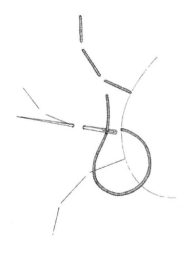

List of suppliers

Free State
Needlewoman
Bloemfontein
051 - 444 5191

Mpumalanga
Bhabha's Cash Store
Ermelo
017 - 8197014

Stitchcraft
Nelspruit
013 - 7523441

North West
J & R Handelaars
Orkney
018 - 4734353

Rustenburg Singer
Rustenburg
014 - 5921231

Eastern Cape
Craft Gallery
Beacon Bay
043 - 7482419

Little Angel & Trousseau
Newton Park
041 - 3639943

Pied Piper
Newton Park
041 - 3651616

Northern Cape
Wolsentrum
Kimberley
053 - 8327542

Namibia
Wool 'n Things
Swakopmund
09264 - 64402674

Elsana Sew & Knit
Windhoek
09264 - 61238649

KwaZulu-Natal
Nimble Fingers
Kloof
031 - 7646283

Busy Needles
Morningside
031 - 3120013

Elna
Shelly Beach
03931 - 50624

Silks & Ribbons
Hillcrest
031 - 7655328

Thimbles & Threads
Hilton
033 - 3431966

Stitchcraft Centre
Umhlanga
031 - 5615822

Patches
Amanzimtoti
031 - 9036574

Gauteng
Brooklyn Wool Shop
Brooklyn
012 - 4604504

Stitch Talk
Centurion
012 - 6632035

The Image
Lynnwoodridge
012 - 3611737

Naaldwerkmandjie
Brits
012 - 2527085

Nadine's Needlework
Die Wilgers
012 - 8074329

Ellen Du Toit
Montana Park
012 - 5487111

Pins & Needles
Gezina
012 - 3359124

Die Werksmandjie
Wierda Park
012 - 6540388

Cross Stitch Connexion
Floradale
011 - 7932693

Threads
Linden
011 - 8884414

Habby & Lace
Vereeniging
016 - 4225400

Pin Cushion
Benmore
011 - 4854327

The Stitchery
Bedfordview
011 - 6167509

De Spinnerinnen
Kempton park
011 - 9724538

Pin Cushion
Wilro Park
011 - 7641549

Cheryl's
Springs
011 - 3625683

Truwish Trading
Weltevreden Park
011 - 7680012

Busy Hands
Atlasville
011 - 3951065

Aladdins Cave
Boksburg
011 - 8234589

Western Cape
Durbanville Needlecrafters
Durbanville
021 - 9757361

Harriett Habbs
Meadowridge
021 - 7124140

Orion Knitting
Cape Town
021 - 4616941

Knitting Nook
Somerset West
021 - 8523044

Cross Stitch Cottage
Bergvliet
021 - 7131709

Stitch Witchery
Hermanus
028 - 3123002

Woolworld International
Salt River
021 - 4484004

Crosspatches
Milnerton
021 - 5519638

Mama's Wool & Habby
Diep River
021 - 7124573

Quiltalk
George
044 - 8732947

Die Wolnessie
Noorder Paarl
021 - 8726281

DMC Creative World (SA)
160 Sir Lowry Road
Cape Town
Tel. 021 461-9482
Fax 021 461-9575
Email: info@dmc-creativeworld.co.za
Website:
www.dmc-cw.com/
www.dmc-usa.com

Supplier of plain white cotton linen
ACG Manufacturers,
23 Sussex Street
Woodstock
021 447-3147
Email: acg@iafrica.com
Website: www.acg.co.za